A Little Light

on Angels

A Little Light on Angels

Diana Cooper

FINDHORN
Press

First published by Findhorn Press 1996
Reprinted many times

ISBN 1-899171-51-7

British Library Cataloguing-in-Publication Data.
A catalogue record for this book is available
from the British Library.

Set in Times by Findhorn Press
Cover design by Thierry Bogliolo
Cover illustration "Angelic Light" © 2002 Emery Bear

Printed and bound by WS Bookwell, Finland

Published by

Findhorn Press

305a The Park, Findhorn
Forres IV36 3TE
Scotland, UK
tel 01309 690582
fax 01309 690036
email info@findhornpress.com
findhornpress.com

Contents

To Jenny

and to the angels with love and thanks

My Introduction to Angels

I suppose I had never really thought very much about angels. Coming as I did from a family where religion was an embarrassing subject and religious people were considered to be slightly suspect, this is not surprising.

My father was a scientist turned businessman and my mother a nurse. They were down-to-earth, logical people, who dismissed the psychic, spiritual and religious as airy fairy nonsense.

As a child, I learned through constant reinforcement that there were three forbidden subjects of conversation in society — money, politics and religion! To me, angels definitely came into the last category.

So it came as a considerable shock one day when I was thirteen and my mother announced that she intended to take my brother Nigel and me to church! To the best of my knowledge I had never been inside one. She said that our religious education had been totally neglected and she was about to rectify that. Nigel and I were both horrified. My mother dressed up in her best clothes and virtually dragged us there. We went sullenly, returned sullenly and the experiment was never repeated. I don't remember the experience, only the sense of confusion and anger I felt. The rules of life seemed to have suddenly changed.

It was when I was seventeen that I had my first and, for many years, only psychic experience and of course I couldn't tell anyone. My boyfriend went to his class party. He was in the year above me at school and his former girlfriend was there. I was at home having my hair washed by my mother in the kitchen, as one did in those days. Suddenly, although I was in the kitchen going through all the motions of talking to my mother as she washed my hair, at the same time I was in the room at the party watching everything that was going on. I was watching my boyfriend kissing his former girlfriend who was sitting on his knee. I felt devastated. Never for a moment did I doubt my experience. As far as I was concerned I was there. I could see everyone and everything in the room.

Next day when he called for me, I greeted him with, "How could you!" Even stranger, he never asked me how or what I knew. We both just knew that I knew.

Life moved inexorably on with ups and downs. I married and had three children. Those years of motherhood, despite the challenges were very happy times. We lived overseas for many years in a materialistic environment.

Then came a very black time. My marriage was in ruins. During this period the children went to boarding school and I felt my role in life had evaporated. When my husband and I returned to live in England, I knew no one. I rattled around alone in a big house with my thoughts going round and round in dark circles. I knew I had to get away, get divorced and find a way to make a home for myself and the children. Somehow I had to earn a living but I had no skills and my confidence level was zero. I was at rock bottom.

That was the moment of deep despair at which I had my first spiritual experience. As I have described in other books, a 'being' lifted me from my suicidal state and took me on a journey round the Universe. The being told me I was a 'teacher'.

I have always called him a 'being of light'. I accept now he was an angel — a beautiful golden angel. But my mind was so closed to angels, for they belonged to religion, that I could not call him an angel, even though he looked like a traditional angel in a picture — although I don't remember any wings. He seemed to fly by gliding through the air or sometimes by zooming very fast, rather like superman.

After this spiritual experience I became interested in spirit guides and learnt to talk to mine and occasionally see them as I became more clairvoyant. Spirit guides are evolved beings in the spirit world, who have usually, but not always, had an incarnation in a physical body on planet Earth. Out of great love and compassion for us they volunteer to guide us and help us with our spiritual growth.

Angels help us with our evolution.

I passionately wanted to become a healer and spiritual teacher. Over the next twelve years my life changed completely. I moved onto a spiritual path, though not a religious one. Now I recognise that all religions are pathways up the spiritual mountain. I accept all religions but belong to none.

Although I was aware from time to time of angels, I communicated first and foremost with my spirit guides. In these years I had many psychic and spiritual experiences.

Then one summer evening I was lying in the bath, soaking in the soft warmth of the bubbly water and contemplating my forthcoming Healing and Psychic Development class. I requested spiritual guidance, asking "What is this class about." Suddenly a voice, or more precisely a powerful clear thought in my head said, "You are to introduce them to healing with angels."

Totally startled I exclaimed, "But I don't know anything about healing with angels."

The voice responded, "Yes, you do. It's just not conscious yet."

"Oh," I said, "But I can't do that on the first class of the new term. Some of them haven't been before."

The answer was straightforward: "Who's running the class — your ego or your higher guidance?"

I took the point and asked, "Well, what's the difference between healing with guides, spiritual healing and angelic healing?"

The voice said, "Angels will lift you both to God." I presumed this meant both the healer and the person being healed. Without pause the voice continued, "You need a solid golden space to invite the angels into. Make it."

The communication terminated. Stunned, I jumped out of the bath and, wrapped in a towel, wrote down what had happened. I assumed any further information I needed would be given to me before the class started — and I was right.

CHAPTER 1

What Are Angels?

"What exactly are angels?" I asked.

My angelic instructor told me that angels are high spiritual beings. He said that Source (or God) appoints angels as guides, protectors and helpers for His creation and uses them as His messengers.

Most humans are less highly evolved spirits, who are in a physical body for this experience on Earth.

Everyone and everything is made up of vibrations. The heavier the vibration, the denser the object, which is why chairs, tables and humans can be seen and felt.

Angels have a lighter, faster vibration, so they are usually invisible to us humans.

They are androgynous beings beyond the need for sexuality as their masculine and feminine aspects are perfectly in balance. When a perfect balance of the masculine and feminine energies is achieved in human beings of either sex, they are beyond sexual desire. Only very evolved humans reach this level which is why celibacy is so difficult for most humans. Those who *strive* to be celibate clearly are not ready.

Where are angels in the spiritual hierarchy? Generally they are on a much higher level than we are, though just like humans they vary in their spiritual growth according to the level of enlightenment they have reached.

Human are evolving on one pathway and angels on another, so a human would only rarely become an angel or vice versa.

My angelic instructor told me that some angels are here to serve and help humankind. Dogs, cats and horses often serve humans too and so do dolphins, yet they are also on their own separate evolutionary path.

It would not normally serve a human soul to return to Earth as a dog, nor would it serve a dolphin's growth to become a human. So angels, dolphins, humans, dogs and other creatures usually evolve on their own pathways and part of their growth takes place as they interact with other species.

I was not aware until I saw and talked to the angels that there are many different kinds of angels, just as there are many races of humans, each learning and growing in its own way. There are angels who dedicate themselves to healing, others to peace and others to promoting love.

An angel comes to each couple at their marriage ceremony. The task of these angels is to help the couple to stay together. Even after a married couple splits up, their angel is still trying to bring them together. This is one reason why we need a divorce ceremony, so that the angel can be released to do other work.

And yes, we do all have a guardian angel at birth who stays near us. Of course, just like our spirit guides, they can only feel as close as we allow them to. Often they cannot get through the turbulent vibrations of our emotions to reach us and enfold us as they would like.

There are small angels, who look after small tasks, and enormous angels with inconceivably vast energy, who oversee great universal projects.

Of course, you will find angels round churches and cathedrals. They are also present whenever people gather together for religious or spiritual purposes. Angels gather at power points on the planet. These are often places of great beauty.

There are huge angels in charge of the vast mountain ranges, forests, stars and suns. There are enormous angels out in space.

Throughout the ages, even in primitive times, artists consciously or unconsciously have tuned into these awarenesses and depicted all the different kinds of angels in pictures and sculptures.

And angels do sing. They are not called choirs of angels by chance. The mystics and spiritual masters throughout history must have seen and heard them, and passed the information on to those who were ready to hear. Angels create divine celestial music, mostly sounds which are beyond the human auditory range. Nevertheless, the heavenly sounds affect us, uplift, inspire and heal us. These sounds touch the very cells of our being and change us whether we are aware of it or not.

The very presence of angels amongst us opens the gates of our consciousness to higher and greater possibilities. And there are more amongst us now than at any previous time in history. The reason for this is that planet Earth has reached a critical point. We have despoiled our planet and surrounded it with an almost impenetrable force of negativity. The Creator has decreed that this cannot continue. We are not to be allowed to destroy the beautiful Earth. This would cause an imbalance in the Universe.

So now humans must raise their consciousness to a level where they honour the Earth, nature, all species of animals and each other — or they must leave.

Angels are flocking here now
to help us all rise in consciousness.

Chapter 2

Angels Are Waiting to Help

Angels have such great love that they respond when we send out cries from the depth of our soul. They also have great compassion for planet Earth, which is why they are appearing in such numbers to offer their help in these times of turbulence, distress and change.

I received the following letter from Patricia O'Flaherty who writes about an incident which occurred during a period of deep and profound unhappiness.

I was sitting alone in the night, sobbing and feeling so alone and wretched, when I suddenly 'heard', "You are not alone. We're here", and became aware of a host of kindly angelic forces in the room with me, warm and loving and moving quietly about, all around me. It cheered me and consoled me and since then, I realise we never are as alone as we perceive ourselves to be.

If our need is great enough, angels will be there to comfort, guide and sometimes even help us physically.

In *The Power of Inner Peace*, I tell the story of a friend of mine who I call Barry in the book. He had been working tremendously long hours to maintain his business. Night after night he drove home in a state of exhaustion, hardly able to keep his eyes open. One night the inevitable happened and just before he reached a busy major roundabout, he fell asleep at the wheel. When he opened his eyes with a start, he had negotiated the roundabout and was driving down the road.

In the seat beside him sat an angel, holding the steering wheel and guiding the car. As soon as he woke, the angel disappeared, leaving him feeling amazed and awed.

I believe that we are constantly being protected by our guardian angels and other spiritual helpers. How else could we, with our limited mortal senses, race down motorways at immense speed and miss each other?

Usually angels are invisible to us because they vibrate on a level beyond the range of human vision. Sometimes we can raise our consciousness sufficiently to see them. On other occasions, because we are in a relaxed or sleepy state, the veil between the worlds thins and we see them.

Most often we simply sense their presence and the impulse of energy from nowhere which helps us. As I was writing this chapter a friend was telling me of her mother, who is a very cautious and down-to-earth person. She was struggling to lift an impossibly heavy wardrobe. Suddenly there was a warm rush of air and she felt the wardrobe being lifted by unseen hands. She 'knew' it was an angel.

There are many references in the Bible to angels coming to people bringing messages during sleep. This still happens but many refer to these visitations simply as dreams — a figment of our imagination. How the higher spiritual worlds must wonder at us humans!

A friend of mine was terrified of flying. When she did try to face her fear, she had a terrifying and debilitating panic attack on the plane. For years, this had stopped her from travelling as she would like to do.

We asked for spiritual help for her, knowing that help will always come when we ask, whether we recognise it and accept it or not.

That night she dreamt that she was on a plane which was

being held up by a huge golden angel. She woke knowing she had been told that it was completely safe for her to travel. She is now a confident frequent flyer.

Sometimes angels even come to us and give us healing during our sleep state. A young woman called Sharon wrote and told me of her healing experience.

Her right knee had become quite painful and she did not know why. She had been to her doctor, who had examined it and given her some medication. She went to bed without taking the medication, planning to start it in the morning.

That night she dreamt that she was lying on her stomach and her legs were weightless. They just floated up. They were still attached to her body and were a little way off the ground. This was a lovely sensation. Then golden hands, just hands, were massaging both of her legs. This too felt wonderful.

The next morning her knee felt much better and over the next couple of days the pain went completely. She never needed the medication.

It will be a different world
when we all call in angels
to help us with our healing.

CHAPTER 3

Spiritual Experiences

Lesley came to my Life Purpose workshop and shared this story of the spiritual experience which set her on a pathway, seeking and searching for the truth.

Three years earlier she had a very emotional and traumatic year of multiple personal losses. As she reeled under shock after shock, she sat and tried to work out the meaning of life. This is what she wrote to me about what subsequently happened.

A week later, while I was sleeping in the early hours of morning, I was awoken by a very bright 'white light'. It was like nothing I had ever seen before on Earth — so bright it 'lit' the whole of my bedroom up. It was not a normal light. I had never encountered something like this before!

It did not make me squint like the sun or car headlights. It was a radiating, bright, 'pure white' light (not blinding but 'glowing') and it was giving out this beautiful warm feeling of love, as if to tell me not to be afraid. I kept looking at this 'being of light' and it made me feel so loved and seemed to say, "You know what I'm here for — believe in me."

I remember waiting to see if I was going to get a

message, and what was going to happen next. The next thing I remember I saw myself looking down from the ceiling at my body in bed. It was incredible. Then before I knew it, I was back in my body in bed, pulling the duvet cover over my head.

It was amazing. I could not forget it, so I started reading books and found out I had seen the 'being of light' and had an out-of-body experience.

Whenever humans are visited by angels, they report an overwhelming feeling of love and peace. Angels do come to reassure us and give us the impetus to move forward.

I often find that when I share my spiritual experiences with people they respond by sharing theirs. On one occasion I was chatting to a young man who told me that he had been in the depth of despair at the break up of a relationship. It was as if his whole heart and soul had been torn apart and he could see no future. All he could see was blackness and he remained in the darkness of this pit for a long time.

Then one night he was looking bleakly out of the window at a tree. Gradually the tree became lighter and lighter until he could only see a radiant light with a face in it. He had a sense of peace and for the first time felt it was possible to live again. From that moment he began to pick up the threads of his life again. He was sure the face was that of his guardian angel.

Angels always radiate peace and love.

CHAPTER 4

Guardian Angels

Our guardian angel is with us throughout all our lives. It comes to us at birth. No one walks their path on planet Earth alone. If only we knew how much help there is around us in the spirit world, we would not feel so vulnerable and alone. Often it is only at times of crisis that we become aware of the presence of this help.

Mary Miller wrote to me of her son's experience with his guardian angel.

My angel story goes back to 1980 when my son started to drive. One night when he had not arrived home by midnight I was over overanxious for his safety. Then an inner voice from wherever prompted me to put his guardian angel on duty. Immediately my anxiety was replaced by a sound sleep.

At breakfast the following morning my son told me of a strange experience on his way home. Within a mile from home he nodded off to sleep. Then he heard a strange voice call his name — in his words — 'not yours. Mam or Dad's or any voice I know. But I will certainly recognise it, should I ever hear it again.'

To this day we are both convinced it was his guardian angel.

Needless to say, I am on very good terms with angels ever since. May the Divine Assistance remain always with us.

I love this story that Mary shared. It shows how we are all linked so deeply. If every mother who worried about her child would ask the child's guardian angel to protect it — and then relax and trust the protection, the world would be a lighter and safer place.

Most parents think they are being good parents when they worry about their children. They are not. Worry is a heavy, dense, negative vibration. When we direct it with force towards our beloved child, who is psychically linked to us, we open our child to disease, danger and negative influences. Black, brooding fear and worry energy can make a sensitive child ill.

When we send love, healing and positive thoughts to our child, we surround that child with a protective, joyous force. If we also ask our child's guardian angel to protect him or her, our love energy opens the way for the guardian angel to link more closely to the child.

Of course, we can do this for anyone, whether a friend or a stranger. Love is the energy that opens the hearts of others and we direct the love energy with our thoughts. When we send pure rays of love to people, the angelic forces can link into them to activate miracles. It is even more powerful if we direct the angels to help.

Listen to your intuition and send love to people in need, in danger, pain or grief. If you pass a hospital, ask the healing angels to help those in need. Your loving intercession allows the angels to get closer and heal more effectively.

Angels heal animals too. If you know of an animal in distress, ask an angel to help it. It will speed the animal's recovery.

When you think of a war zone, do not focus on the bad things happening there. This energises the darkness. Instead picture light going into the area. Ask the angels to help the people there. Your prayers become pathways of light for the angels to enter and help.

If we hear, read about or see bad news in the media, we can pause for a moment and send light to the area. This assists more than we are aware of. The love and light we send can avert disasters, can help and heal others. Every one of us plays an important role on the planet. You may think your little bit makes no difference but when added to energy others are sending, it creates a vast wave of light which can help to make massive changes to heal people and places.

Evil, or the terrible feeling of being separate from Source, as I prefer to see it, is afraid of light. Sending waves of light to the minds of 'evil' people and leaders, who place personal power above the growth of their people, will wash out the need for control and abuse and allow freedom to return.

When we send loving thoughts to others,
we create bridges of light for Angels to walk along.

CHAPTER 5

Angels Are in Service

After the angels appeared to me, I was very excited about my Healing and Psychic Development class and hoped that I could keep my vibration steady enough for them to come close.

My angel instructor told me that angels work on a golden ray and indeed I saw the healing angels as whitish gold in colour. They were the same colour as the angelic being who came to me in my moment of soul despair, and were about seven feet tall.

He said, "Gold is the colour of wisdom and truly unconditional love. When you are healing with these angels, it is a golden energy.

Angelic energy has a sunshine warmth and no angel will ever make you feel cold when it is near you."

He added that angels are in service and that when you work with angelic energy you identify yourself with being in service.

So at the class we sat quietly and imagined ourselves filling the room with gold light until we were in a solid golden space.

Before the class started I had been told to ask everyone to stroke their own aura with their hands. After this we were to invite angels to stroke our auras. This would give us the opportunity to feel the loving energy of the angelic beings waiting to help us all.

So I asked everyone to feel their aura with their hands and then stroke it. We can all do this by gradually bringing our hands closer to our bodies until we feel the slight resistance or tingling feeling of the edge of our aura. It is a practical way to smooth over any holes or uneven places in our auras so that we are more protected. Most people experienced it as calmly soothing.

Our aura is our protective electromagnetic shield. It is created by our thoughts. Wishy-washy thoughts mean that we have a weak aura which does not protect us from the actions or thoughts of others. Strong, positive and loving thoughts ensure a solid protective aura. Negative thoughts make holes in our auras, while if we are in shock, our aura often disappears and we are very vulnerable to outside forces.

Most of us have seen pictures of saints, gurus and holy people with beautiful golden halos around their heads or with golden auras round their bodies. These are the colours of their pure and spiritual thoughts as seen by those with eyes to see auras.

I and many of the class participants could see a ring of angels round the room, drawn near in response to our expectation, waiting to help. Each person in the class invited in an angel to stroke their aura. This proved to be a very different experience from smoothing their own aura. It felt very powerful and several people burst into tears.

One of the class members shared what had happened to her. She told us that she had had a blinding headache all day and desperately wanted an angel to come to her. She thought an angel would help her headache but none would come to her. Instead a cherub played around her. It was smiling and absolutely delightful but it kept swishing about above her head.

She kept saying to it, "Stroke my aura," but it just smiled and played above her head. The more frustrated she became, the more the cherub smiled and wafted over her. However, when the cherub waved and left at the end of the exercise, her headache had gone completely!

There were several experienced healers in this class, so I asked them to let go of all preconceptions, empty their minds and put their hands on the aura of the person they were working with, allowing the angels to work through them. Most of them were astonished. They felt the power of the angels flowing through them.

A similar thing happens when we open ourselves up as a channel for spiritual healing. The clearer a channel we are the more divine healing energy flows through us. However the healing with the angels felt quite different. It actually felt golden.

Here is what one of the participants wrote to me afterwards.

When you introduced us to angels at the healing class, I could really feel a very light but powerful energy. I particularly enjoyed going with the angels and the lady I was healing up to Source for healing energy. Since then I have asked the angels to come to me every day. Although I can't see them, I can always feel their warm, loving presence and they have seen me through some rough times! I asked them to be there when I came for a session with you and they came and, I feel, performed the most miraculous healing!

Angels heal in a light way.

CHAPTER 6

The Healing Power of Forgiveness

I first met Lynfa Davies at one of my Healing with Angels workshops. I noticed her immediately as she radiated a glow of warmth and happiness.

During the course of the workshop she shared this story. She had been raped when she was thirteen. Her marriage had broken up. So had a very abusive relationship which followed. The pain around these memories was pretty intense, so much so that counselling and similar therapies seemed very threatening.

She realised that she had a choice. She could continue to exist with the pain and hurt or she could find a way of letting it go and forgiving, so that she could live again.

She chose rebirthing because it is much less intellectual and mind-based than many therapies and soon decided that it is indeed possible to heal anything — however painful. With this intention she worked with her rebirther. This is what she wrote about her subsequent experience.

Following this decision, I started to get what I thought was indigestion — really severe pains around my heart. During the next session, I was breathing as usual and I suddenly heard and felt wings just above my head. Everything became very calm and in my mind's eye I saw large, white wings around me. I felt completely engulfed by them, completely safe and then I saw a man's face looking down at me. He looked rather like the angels from Wim Wender's film "Wings of Desire" — fierce, strong and very gentle.

He told me that my heart was broken, and that it had been for a long time, and that he had come to put it together again. I felt a very warm feeling in and around my heart — an enormous energy and also a feeling of peace and knowing that things were OK and I was safe. At the end of the session the pain had gone, and I can now talk about being raped very much more easily, with no pain.

I am a pretty down-to-earth sort of person — but since this session I have been using angel cards and feel very protected and cared for, which is definitely a new thing for me.

When we put out our intentions and are open to all possibilities miracles happen. Annie Rossiter shared this story of what happened to her after a workshop.

I had been to one of your workshops, Diana. My father had abused me as a child and I was looking at why I had chosen the parents I had. It was while I was doing this that I realised how much anger I was holding onto towards him.

You helped me to let that go. That in itself was quite an amazing experience. I got home and felt shaken but not unpleasantly so. I just needed to meditate and be still and quiet. Having let go of the anger, I felt empty. Although you had got me to breathe in love, I wanted more. I needed love to fill my emptiness where the anger had been.

I lay on the bed and became very quiet. I began to hear a noise, a very soft noise, like the rustling of feathers. Then in my mind I saw white angels with beautiful white wings and I had a great sense of love filling me.

This had a profound effect on me. The anger is not there any more. Before I was blaming my father for my life. Now all the blame has gone.

Angels can fill our hearts with love.

CHAPTER 7

Angels and Children

Children, before their memory banks close down in the heavy vibration of planet Earth, often communicate with the spirit world and they can frequently recall their past lives. One mother told me her three-year-old said to her one day, "You know Mummy, it's funny having these legs. They were brown before."

Many children, especially those who have no siblings or who are lonely, play with invisible friends. These friends, invisible to adult eyes, are perfectly real and visible to those little ones who still have eyes to see the spiritual realms. The invisible ones are, of course, children from the spirit world.

These children are also open to seeing fairies and angels. In a child, the right brain is naturally open to such experiences. When our right brain is developed, we are more intuitive, psychic and imaginative. This is the side of our brain which governs healing, mediumship, creative and artistic work. However, in our culture, we lean heavily towards logical thinking and numerate school work, with emphasis on competition and success. When, at the age of five, our children enter such an education system, inevitably their natural intuition, creativity and imagination shut down. Between the ages of five and ten, most children cease to commune with spirit children, fairies and angels.

It will transform planet Earth when we honour the equal

development of the right and left brain. Then we will have superhumans, accessing much greater potential and living at a higher level of awareness.

Jeanne Slade told me her story in her lovely, lilting Welsh accent. Like so many Celts, she is a natural psychic and has been for as long as she can remember. The eldest of four children she was born and brought up in a cottage in the heart of Wales. The number of the cottage was 33. Every house number has a vibration. She told me that the number 11 is especially good for the development of intuition, clairvoyance and psychic ability. A house number 22 has the vibration of unlimited potential and to live in a house numbered 33 means that all things are possible!

As a dreamy, psychic child she saw and communed with angels. Her mother lacked understanding and often sent her to her room, where she spent much time alone. When she spoke of the angels to her grandmother, the older woman told her not to tell lies! It was very confusing for the child to be told that her reality was a falsehood. Nevertheless she continued to gain comfort from the presence of her guardian angel.

Then when she was seven years old, the quiet, sensitive child was abused by her teacher at school. In the way of children she thought that somehow it must be her fault, that somehow she must be bad for such a thing to happen and she did not tell anyone. From that moment she never saw her guardian angel again. In the trauma of losing her innocence and her spiritual support, she suppressed the memories of the abuse and of the angels.

As an adult during therapy full memory of the abuse returned. She finally exorcised the pain in the only possible way, by genuine forgiveness of the perpetrator. At the moment of forgiveness she exclaimed, "Oh, I can see my angel again." She realised that as a child she felt that she had been bad and the abuse must have been her fault. Therefore she felt that she did not deserve to have a guardian angel. Because of this belief she could not see it any more.

Jeanne's daughter, who is a practising clairvoyant, was able to communicate with Jeanne's grandmother, who had passed over and was in spirit. The grandmother told her that she had sent a guide to help Jeanne with the regression because she felt very guilty about her childhood.

It transpired that Jeanne's grandmother was also psychic. When she was telling Jeanne as a child not to tell lies about the angels, she could in fact see them herself.

Presumably when she was on Earth, her grandmother thought she would be helping the child to be more 'normal and acceptable' if she denied the presence of the angels. From the higher perspectives of the spirit world, she realised the damage she had done and tried to make amends.

Now, although Jeanne has not 'seen' the angels since, she has felt and experienced the enormous love of their presence.

Such stories from childhood often remind me of the tale of The Emperor's Clothes. In this story a pair of villains told the courtiers that they were spinning magic cloth. If the buyers were honest and worthy, they would be able to see the splendid material, but if the buyers should be stupid and dishonest, then the material would be invisible. No-one wished to admit that they could not see the expensive clothes for which they were being measured. The emperor himself pretended he could see his new clothes because he thought everyone would realise he was stupid and dishonest if he admitted he could not see them. So he went out into the town without clothes, while everyone pretended to admire them in case they should be considered the stupid and dishonest ones. Only a child called out, "The Emperor isn't wearing any clothes."

Where many an adult will deny that they can see an angel
for fear of being ridiculed,
a child in its innocence will speak the truth.

CHAPTER 8

Peace Angels

I had never even heard of peace angels but when I saw them I knew immediately who they were. They were larger than the healing angels and a different colour. These beautiful luminous beings were creamy white and fluffy with large, soft wings. I can't describe them in any other way. They were warm and felt feathery and incredibly calm.

A few days after I first became aware of these angels, I was running a course on inner peace. Presumably that is why they appeared to me. One of the participants, a most pleasant and charming man, worked in the city. I felt sure that he had come to an inner peace workshop to de-stress himself and would have no concept of higher spiritual realms. During one exercise I became aware of one of the peace angels standing behind him, enfolding his solar plexus with her wings. For an instant I considered whether or not to say anything. I certainly did not want to frighten him. On the other hand, I did not want to miss an opportunity which might be important for him. So I said to him that a peace angel had her wings round him and if he cared to lean back into her she would hold him. Without hesitation he did so and afterwards told me that it was a wonderful comforting experience. He felt inspired and delighted by it.

I do hope he took the peace back into the city.

A few months later I was again about to teach a weekend

course on inner peace. I was in my local pool thinking about the course as I swam and my mind must have become relaxed and receptive for suddenly a voice said:

"We want you to impart an important message to those whom we've brought together this weekend. *Peace must be spread and it can only start within individuals who are ready to forgo their power struggle with others. Peace is surrender to spirit, not proving you are better than another.*

"Impress on each one to make a corner of their home into a peace corner. This doesn't mean candles or crystals or rituals. It means a space in which you think only peaceful thoughts. It may be as small as one chair in the house but having chosen the spot never approach it unless your thoughts are centred and peaceful. That little corner is like an acorn of peace. It will sprout and grow through slender sapling into vast protective oak which will fill and protect your home.

"Start by planting one peace acorn in your home. Then little by little plant others in other places. With other like minded souls choose a spot. It may be a telephone box in your High Street or a corner of your town. If each of you enter this small space whenever you are near with peace thoughts only, even if it is only for a moment, you are planting and nurturing a peace place.

"Many, but not all, trees are anchors for peace on planet Earth. If you are centred and calm and you pass such a tree, pause, breathe peace out to the tree and breathe peace back in from it. This will help to strengthen the peace points on the planet and will help you to become an anchor point for peace — someone who can spread peace."

It is spiritual law that whatever we focus on increases. The peace angel impressed on me,

Focus on peace and fear will dissolve.
Focus on love and hate will disappear.
Focus on joy and grief will evaporate.
Cultivate flowers and weeds cannot take hold.

CHAPTER 9

Spiritual Oil

One message from the angelic peace bearers was, *"You cannot be at peace while you give anyone or anything power over you. If anyone has any influence over your thoughts and feelings — to the extent that they affect you, you are not at peace."*

When we are in a solid unbroken aura, we are totally protected and, of course, no one can influence us. If our aura is broken at any point because of our negative thoughts, we are vulnerable and then it is difficult to feel peaceful. An aura made strong by our own powerful and positive thoughts is impregnable. Then we feel safe.

Angels can and do come in and stroke our auras if we ask them to. This immediately strengthens the aura and helps to protect us.

Again and again they tell me that they are waiting to help but we must ask them to. We can even ask them to help others and they will willingly do so. They respond to our energy. If you are driving down the road and you hear an ambulance siren, ask for extra angelic help for the person in need. You do not know what force for good you set in motion.

The peace angels reminded me about a recent client whom I shall call George and added the reminder that they were always ready and willing to work in this way with people if only we invite them to.

George was a very good man, spiritual and well-intentioned, but in turmoil. He felt powerless and was full of feelings of anger and rage. Negative emotions make holes in our aura and because his protective aura was full of holes he had no energy and had become physically ill. He was seeking the cause of this problem.

He told me that in a past life under torture, he had betrayed his people. When I started working with him, I closed my eyes and immediately saw a picture of him with hundreds of cords, like hosepipes, attached to him.

When I followed one of these cords, I saw at the other end a crowd of people surrounded in darkness. The dark energy was the fear and anger of those people he had betrayed. Each one of them still had a cord hooked into him. Even now their fear and rage was flowing through it like sludge through a pipe.

Of course, if his aura had been solid and unbroken, these cords could not have penetrated his space but his guilt and anger let them in. Whether these people were incarnate or not, these lines were still active. Also active were the lines of anger which attached him to his enemies.

Because all these unhealthy cords were piercing his aura, he could never make it strong and peaceful, so he was vulnerable to negative influences.

The angel said to me, "As you know, we angels were waiting, longing to help. All week before he came for his session with you, he felt the importance of it but he didn't know why. It was because you were calling on us — angels of light — to help.

When you first asked for grace, you set powerful wheels in motion — and the dispensing of a spiritual oil. We angels were so joyful to be asked — as you saw. While you held the energy, we were able to release all those cords and take those souls into the light."

When it is time for someone to die, angels do help them onto the next stage of their journey. Our prayers greatly help.

Certain souls get stuck, either because they are too attached to the material world or because they are attached by negative emotions such as lust, greed or anger. Angels also help these souls to make the transition but often they need our energy to intercede. General and specific prayers to help such souls are much appreciated by the Universe.

In freeing the souls who had been attached to George the angels allowed him to become stronger, healthier and happier.

Many of us constantly complain about what we do not have or what we do not want. Spiritual law says, "Where thought goes, energy flows". So when we complain and grumble we get more of what we don't want. When we focus on what we do want, it increases.

When we keep saying thank you for what we do have, those good things increase immeasurably. If children say thank you dully and automatically for something or grab for more, their parents feel disinclined to give. But if children, glowing with delight, say thank you from the heart, their parents want to give more and more.

The Universal energy is the same. Saying thank you from the heart for the good things in our lives, for the qualities we have, for the gifts and talents bestowed on us allows angels to bring more and more abundance to us. It used to be called counting your blessings.

Saying thank you cleanses and clarifies our aura.
It is another spiritual oil
and draws abundance into our lives.

CHAPTER 10

Angels of Ceremony and Ritual

Wherever a contract or vow is made, whenever a bond is signed, there is at least one angel present.

If anything is celebrated with 'pomp and ceremony' there are literally hosts of angels participating. They help to build up the power of the event. They help to keep the legalities binding.

At the exchange of vows, the contract is recorded in the akashic record and an angel comes in to oversee the project. In the case of a marriage, for example, an angel will stay with the couple and become the whispered voice of conscience and wise guidance to try to keep them together. However, we always have free will. If the marriage was one of convenience or if there was no real commitment by either party, it is not noted by spirit as a marriage and no angel will be allocated. So the intention of the vow is also a relevant factor.

At a wedding celebration there are many angels singing, rejoicing and filling the nuptuals with love and heavenly laughter. Of course, there are weddings where the participants are so anxious and out of harmony that they are not touched by the angelic energy. Nevertheless, the angelic hosts are present at the ceremony waiting to lift the vibration if the families will allow it.

If only we humans could open up more to their presence

how much lighter and more fun life would be. The state of being in love is a light state, so when we are in love we are open to the influence of the celestial helpers, whether or not we can see or sense them. This fills lovers with a wonderful sense of joy and elation. With angelic help we see the best in others.

When our relationships get heavy, we close down and are no longer open to receive the help of our angels, who are still patiently waiting. There is so much help available to us if only we will ask and open ourselves up to receive.

At a christening, or its equivalent in other religions, the angels are always present. Again they rejoice at the party afterwards. They bring joy to the occasion and a boost of energy to help the child on its path.

Any landmark on our Earth journey is celebrated by the angels. They come to our birthday parties, anniversaries, graduations, housewarming parties, new job or promotion parties. They are at Christmas parties or Easter ones. They love parties, by which I do not mean drunken orgies, but genuine celebrations where people gather together to enjoy themselves and say thank you.

If we had separation or divorce celebrations, the angels would attend to add their blessing and energy to our new pathway in life. It would make our lives flow more smoothly.

It is wonderful when we honour and rejoice in our birthday. The celestial beings at our birthday celebration give us a boost throughout the year. After all we were offered a special opportunity to come to Earth and it is the anniversary of our arrival. Souls queue up to inhabit a body on planet Earth because the opportunities for spiritual growth are so great here. Every single day we are alive offers us incredible choices to expand our consciousness. There is no other plane in the Universe where souls can grow so quickly. If we realised this and honoured it, we would greet every moment with zest and delight. We would open our eyes each morning with expectation and wonder. How can I grow today? What can I learn today? What challenges can I overcome today? What fears can I conquer? Thank you for this opportunity.

In simpler times all rites of passage were celebrated, even the arrival of spring or coming of the rains. The planting of seeds and the harvesting of crops merited a celebration. The rising sun was greeted with a salutation.

We always hold a meditation evening at full moon in our home and the angels are there lifting and directing the energy. They love the sacred energy of ritual.

Angels are, of course, present and rejoicing at funerals. To those with eyes to see, the discarding of our physical body so that we can move through the door into the Light is a time for rejoicing. They direct our prayers to help in the best possible way the person who is passing, and they sing to aid the spirit of the departed on its journey.

Angels of ceremony and ritual
are present
at all rites of passage.

CHAPTER 11

Angels Light up the Dark

Gerard appeared to have everything to live for, a warm and loving girlfriend, a child he adored and some good friends but he had some dark memories. One day he tried to commit suicide. His family were considerably shaken and persuaded him to come for help.

He did come for one session which helped him to feel at peace for six weeks. Then something happened which brought up old childhood memories again. He fell back into depression and panic and came for a second appointment.

This time I could strongly feel the presence of the angels who were in the room, so I talked to him about them. After that I regressed him back into his childhood and this time we invited the angels in to help with the healing.

Suddenly a ring of angels surrounded him and poured pure white light into him. It was quite amazing to watch. They dissolved the hurt and pain of the little abused child which he still carried inside him. He started to sob as he experienced their love and compassion. When he stopped he said he felt absolutely wonderful.

On another occasion I took a young man back into his childhood. Spontaneously he slipped into a past life as a woman where he had been violated. Even though he had incarnated this time as a man, he still held the memory and feelings within his consciousness.

We worked on the dark feelings of rage and shame which had been suppressed in that lifetime and which still needed to be released. A circle of angels appeared and hovered round him. I suggested that he ask them for healing. They held him very gently and he felt them bearing him up and up to higher realms before they healed the hurt.

I know this young man was in crisis over money and had been seeking and searching for healing for years. When he paid at the end of the session, he said, "It has been worth every penny to be taken to heaven."

The gentleness of the angels is something often commented upon. A businessman had a terrible fear of torture. He often visited countries with a reputation for torture and always felt in dreadful danger.

I regressed him to a past life where he was imprisoned in heavy chains and died under torture. As he experienced this, an angel appeared to him and unchained his body. The beautiful compassionate being gave his tortured body healing and took it away *calmly and tenderly*. (Those are his words.) He was very affected by the gentleness of it.

Healing angels are compassionate and gentle.

CHAPTER 12

Angels Heal Our Hearts

Angels are willing and ready to help us. They have drawn close to our planet in large numbers and are waiting to be called on. The only thing that stops them helping is that we are not open to them. They are happy to help us with our relationships.

Ann was very undecided about her life. She didn't know what to do about her relationship. Her boyfriend was suffering from depression and their relationship was rocky.

To my delight angels came into the room and indicated that they were willing to work with her.

I watched two angels put their hands into her heart, filling and smoothing several cracks with healing light. She relaxed as they worked on her. Then they moved to her solar plexus. I saw them pull out grey fluff. Ann told me that they were pulling out dust, like the congealed dust in a dustbin bag. When the angels had pulled out all the grey fluff and passed it to the light, they filled her solar plexus with a lovely golden light and sealed it in.

Then I was shown that she was to go to a hilltop where she could look down on her life. From there she saw that her energy looked brown like rust and her boyfriend was attached to her with sickly green cords. These cords were going into her throat, choking her.

We asked the angels to go in and dissolve the cords with

light, which they did, sending light right into the roots of the cords, so that everything was dissolved. She could feel the strange sensation.

When the cords had all gone, she said she felt odd, as if there was no energy in her body where the cords had been. We all take energy from somewhere. She had been in the habit of plugging into her boyfriend and other people when she needed a boost of energy. Now I suggested that, instead of looking for a fill up of lower energy as she had done in the past, she link into the waiting angels.

As the pure, clear energy entered her, it highlighted for her that she had never had a relationship in which she stood on her own two feet. She had always been co-dependent and leaning. She said in a small voice, "If I'm not vulnerable, I won't be given love."

When I asked her to sense the quality of love she would receive if she were no longer vulnerable and needy, she experienced that she would receive much more wholesome love and respect.

She visualised what her life would be if she maintained and built upon the feeling of wholeness she had, and she felt for the first time a sense of purpose. She felt huge, strong and confident.

The angels stroked her aura to keep these feelings within her auric space, so that she had the opportunity of consolidating the new qualities. When she opened her eyes, she felt that she could move forward in a much stronger way.

A month later she came back to see me again and said that she had had a warm golden feeling of confidence in her solar plexus ever since the angels had worked on her.

She told me that she had always been very jealous of her partner's friends, even his male friends and would throw a wobbly if he went out with them. After the angels sealed strength and confidence into her solar plexus, her feelings changed dramatically.

A few days after the healing from the angels, her partner's ex girlfriend phoned and said she missed him and wanted to meet up with him. Feeling totally relaxed and unconcerned, Ann had passed him the phone and said, "Why don't you take it into the kitchen where you can have a private chat?"

She had felt untroubled while he was talking to his ex girlfriend. And her new confidence was rewarded. When he came back into the room he said, "I told her I was in a committed relationship and I didn't want to meet her."

Angels help us in the highest way for our growth.

Chapter 13

Angels Are Everywhere

At the end of one class, I asked the participants to watch out for angels the following week. I was surprised by the response. It appeared that once we are aware and looking, angels appear at all sorts of moments. This does not necessarily mean ethereal beings flying in the sky!

One person felt really depressed. She walked down a street she had walked down a million times and glanced casually up. Above her, looking down at her, was a stone angel with sunlight shining all over it. She had never seen it before. Suddenly she felt warm and safe.

One of my favourite angel stories was told to me at our next class and was very simple. Eileen had been nursing her dying father for some time and he had finally died. She felt very sad and empty as she took flowers to the cemetery The place was deserted and she stood by the grave for a while reflecting on old memories.

She turned to walk away, wondering where all the helping angels were when a woman appeared from nowhere and walked towards her. The stranger said, "You don't know me, but I know you."

Eileen said, "Oh, who are you?"

"Angela!", the stranger replied and walked away leaving

Eileen feeling amazed and much comforted. She knew that the angels were reminding her they were there.

At the end of another very special healing class, everyone felt touched by the energy that had been flowing through the room. As we linked hands at the end of the session, I became aware that behind each person was standing their guardian angel, with the angels' hands on the persons' shoulders, ready to enfold, support and protect them. I asked everyone to be aware of this.

When each person had time to absorb the wonderful feeling, I suggested they visualise a golden bubble around themselves. Afterwards one participant said, "I physically felt my angel's hands on my shoulders and when you asked us to put the golden bubble round us, it stepped back to allow space for the bubble to go round me."

Angels are always there to help us.

CHAPTER 14

Angels Help Us to Let Go

Debbie arrived to see me in a state of shock. Her mother, with whom she was very close, had been rushed to hospital and was in intensive care where she lay in a coma. Naturally Debbie wanted to wait by her bedside but friends persuaded her to come for her appointment. One of them drove her to my house and waited for her.

No sooner had the session started than angels entered the room. They indicated that she was holding on to her mother and that it was important she detach, or uncord, from her. This would free her mother to decide whether to come back or to pass over. Of course, this felt devastating for Debbie, but she had a high level of spiritual understanding and recognised that it was right.

I relaxed Debbie and asked her to visualise the cords which attached her to her mother. She saw grey chains surrounding them both and we asked the angels to dissolve them. They gently pulled all the chains away, freeing mother and daughter from each other.

When all the chains had been released, Debbie saw that her mother was stronger and she herself felt happy and bigger, as if she had grown.

Later that day, she phoned me to say that, *at the exact moment of uncording, her mother had come off the ventilator and sat up*. She felt that her letting go had been a vital part of this.

A week later her mother died. That week gave them an opportunity to say goodbye properly and I believe that the angels interceded to allow this.

A few days after this a young woman came to me because she could not get away from her family. Her father was an angry bully, who blackmailed her into staying at home by saying that she could never come back if she left. None of the family had been able to escape and they lived in a household of anger, silences and fear.

As she talked about her father, it became very clear that he was holding onto everyone because he was terrified of being left alone. She realised that it was not his wise adult self who was blackmailing and threatening her. When he bullied the family, he was a terrified little five-year-old boy.

For the first time she became aware that her father was desperate about what would happen to him if she left. With that awareness came a tenderness and sense of compassion. Now she understood just how much reassurance and love he really needed.

As I watched, her face softened as her heart opened towards him. She saw that if her father felt she really loved him, he would be quite happy to let her go, knowing that she would always return.

Then an angel took her to look down at the family scene from above. She saw a mass of angry, demanding faces, filled with fear and insecurity. They were all stuck in a black treacly mess and none of them could get out of it. The angel poured golden light into the treacle around her and gradually freed her to swim out of it. We asked the angel to release the rest of the family from the treacle and it did so by pulling out the dark sticky energy and pouring in more gold.

Within a short while her brother left home and she started to feel freer to do what she wanted to do.

Angels are free spirits and will help us to be free too.

CHAPTER 15

Healing with Angels

When I told her that I was writing a book about angels, one of my clients, a beautiful young lady who had been through a great deal of loss and hardship, sent me the following letter about her experiences during our healing sessions.

Angels heal deep wounds

I came to you feeling trapped by fear, and feeling very frustrated. I had spent a lot of time in hospital when I was young and had loads of fears of what might happen to me next.

We were doing some inner child work to empower my stuck child. After I had put my empowered three-year-old into my solar plexus, two angels came in to help. They pulled out a really long, black, thick cord from my throat that went right down into my solar plexus. I was amazed because I could actually feel it happening.

Then we moved on to another incident when I was frightened as a six-year-old. The angels came and helped again. They released black smoke from my solar plexus. Then they lifted my six year old, black with smoke, up to Source. It felt so great that I didn't want to come back!

The session was very powerful and I was very happy that I had so much help around. I felt pleased that there is a way of healing deep wounds and changing frustrating patterns in my life.

Releasing feelings of abandonment

A few weeks later I came to see you again. I had had a terrible week with old emotions surfacing and completely taking hold of me. The main issue was feelings of abandonment — feeling unwanted and unloved. I kept waking up in the early hours of the morning feeling like my heart was tearing apart. The feelings were so intense and uncomfortable I felt like destroying myself to ease the pain. I knew these feelings were from the past and I had done months of inner work on loving myself but I was at my wit's end.

During the session you saw a number of angels with a jug of golden liquid. They smoothed this over my aura and again I was amazed as I could actually feel their energy.

We then did some inner child work during which the angels intervened! They wanted to hold my nine-year-old up to the light. Then they wanted to take me up to Source. You asked me if I wanted to go up to Source as it would mean purification. I was frightened of going but said I would go as I was at the end of my tether!

So I had to breathe in light and breathe out all sorts of things including anger, guilt and jealousy. Then I had an angel on either side and was taken up to Source. On the way up I felt sick. Then I felt really in the depths of depression and despair. Then when I got to Source I was to kneel before the Lords of Karma, who look after the akashic records. They were to let me resolve this with grace.

I had an angel on either side and I could see bright white light. They put a white cross on my forehead and a hand on my heart. My attention was drawn to the white cross because I could feel the warmth and the shape of it in front of my head — and at that moment all those feelings of sickness and depression and the tension in my shoulders and neck just completely washed away!

I saw myself kneeling with the white cross on my forehead. Then I was to come back down. I really wanted to stay and savour the feeling. It was really lovely, special and holy but only lasted for a few seconds.

I was absolutely amazed at the feelings that I had had! At the time you said you had never taken anyone to Source like that before and that I had a lot of help available to me.

Since that session I have never had any of those awful abandonment feelings again and I completely trust the ability of the angels to heal.

Releasing depression

The third spectacular angel healing I had was when I fell into a black hole of depression. It had been going on for two weeks and I tried everything to pull myself out but I kept falling back down that hole.

It was completely engulfing me and affecting my work as everything was out of proportion. At this point I knew the only way out was to call on the angels for help! I came to see you and true to form the angels came along to help!

My small child was in the bottom of a black pit of snakes. The angels removed those snakes, filled the hole in my solar plexus up with golden light and lifted my child up into the light.

It seemed so simple, yet it was incredibly powerful as the depression went away completely straight away!

Since then I have been hooked on angels! I often ask for healing from them and for their help. I have never seen one clearly but have had the impression of a whole group of rainbow-coloured angels lifting me up to the light and I can always feel their warm energy. They have even healed my horse when he was choking.

So thank you very much for introducing me to angels!

She no longer needs to come to me as an intermediary. She can now invite in the angels herself to do the healing.

CHAPTER 16

The Trumpets Blow

Just as there are healing angels, so there are angels of joy, balance, grace, trust and every other conceivable quality.

Because their energies are different, they all look different. They appear in colours in tune with their energy, and their robes are a variety of styles and patterns.

Like any other angels, when directly called upon they will answer our prayers for help. In the new consciousness we will ask for qualities rather than material things to be brought to us.

At one of my workshops I suggested that the participants ask the angels for the qualities they wanted to be brought to them. One lady asked the angels for *protection, clarity, inner peace, direction and health*. She had M.E. and had been ill for years. When we ask we are given. Two weeks later I met her and this is what she told me.

A few days after the workshop I met a friend who gave me a bottle containing a combination of oils for protecting my aura. I did not ask for these oils. She just felt impressed to make them up for me. Amongst those oils were fennel for protection against psychic attack and rosemary for psychic protection and clarity. I felt this was an immediate response to my request for protection and clarity. Almost immediately my mind felt much clearer.

The following day your Inner Peace tape arrived which someone had sent me. I listened and felt calmer and clearer still. I knew that I could use it to find peace until I had it firmly inside me.

Some weeks beforehand I had sent for a clairvoyant reading, asking for direction. This arrived on the same day and I resonated with everything that was said. Later that week I went on a trip to Stonehenge and was given some channelled information about my future. I was told to follow my heart. Then I listened to your Self Worth tape telling me to follow my heart. I picked an angel messenger card, which also said follow your heart.

My health was still proving difficult. A friend telephoned to see how I was. This friend was a nutritionist, who gave me a thorough health check, a reflexology treatment and a supply of vitamins and minerals.

I sent a prayer of thanks to the angels. They had responded to all five of the things I asked for but I still felt very tired and unwell.

Next day she wrote to me with the following story:

Angels have healed me in the past on an emotional level and made miraculous differences, so I thought maybe they could heal me on a physical level and give me grace to release my post viral fatigue! It would certainly be a miracle, as this has been going on for a few years now.

So I lay down to meditate and as I did so, I felt a large angel at my head, holding one hand either side of my head. Obviously the intention was enough to draw the angels close.

I asked to be taken to Source and given grace to release my illness. At Source I was lying down, covered in a white cloth. There were lots of angels around me — at least twenty, and still the angel was at my head. I could see bright golden light shining between the angels who were dressed in white.

I heard trumpets blowing and looked up and there were two angels floating above me. I got the names Cherubim and Seraphim and have since found out they are at the top of the angel hierarchy. At the time I was not even sure if they were angels' names.

I asked why the trumpets were blowing and I was told, "Because you are special."

I asked for grace to release my illness and a Godforce in the form of a white mist came over and through me from my toes right up to my head to release negativity. This happened four times.

Then I was infused with a golden beam of light from head to toe. I could see an amazing bright golden, sparkling beam of light coming to my head but at first it couldn't get in. So the angels used a liquid to clear a channel down my spine. The light, once in, gradually spread around to all the cells of my body. I particularly felt it in the upper body.

I wanted to stay at Source to really allow the healing to start working. I then felt immense heat in my head and particularly around the back of my neck at the top of my spine. The heat was inside me. The angel was still at my head. Then after a few minutes my head completely cleared and I felt really peaceful. It was like a sudden release.

I had a long thin cross of light placed over my body. Then I came down from Source and into my heart centre and into my body. I was told to rest for seven days.

Afterwards I felt really peaceful. All my worries, anxieties and thoughts were gone."

Angels rejoice that we are special.

CHAPTER 17

Angels of Colour

Medical doctors use ultrasound to shake out the negative energy locked into painful joints. They use ultraviolet rays to penetrate and release certain conditions in the body. We know that the use of sound and colour in this way can effectively heal. However, it is a very violent use of sound and colour, rather like taking a mallet to crack a nut.

Every colour has its own vibration and energy which affects us unconsciously even if we are unaware at a conscious level. Bright red will energise us, while green will balance and blue will soothe. Yellow helps us with concentration and indigo will calm the mind. The colours we paint our walls will affect us. We pick colours to wear which reflect our personality or provide something we lack.

In the same way, when appropriate colours are directed towards the healing of the body, they penetrate the cells and energise them or dissolve negative energy. While one disease may respond to one colour, another will be affected by a different colour.

For instance cancers respond to green, which is the colour of the heart centre and we need our own heart centre to be open and relaxed in order to bring this colour through effectively. People in shock or those whose minds need to be calmed respond to indigo. Someone in depression will respond favourably to the warm reds and oranges.

Colour healing is very effective and is becoming more recognised now. Some healers are very intuitive about colour and send the perfect shade to help their patients. Others are not able to see colours very clearly or are not confident that they are selecting the right ones.

What we do not realise is that the angels of colour are always around to help us. Whenever we think a colour and project it onto someone, an angel will be there to help us. If we ask them for help, relax and allow them to take over, we can rest assured that the perfect colours will be chosen by them, so that the patient will get the maximum benefit.

It is then counterproductive to concentrate too hard. Our task is simply to maintain a relaxed focus, so that the angels can work through us.

If we want to visualise the colour ourselves, it is always safe to focus on white light. This includes all the colours of the spectrum, so angels can choose and mix whichever colour the recipient most needs.

White is a very pure, protective colour and when we use white light for protection we are impregnable. We can be certain that the angels are very strongly with us.

I was talking about the power of white light at one of my workshops and a participant shared this story. She is very strongly clairvoyant and has always seen energy around people. At that time she had a job in a shop and once a week had to carry a considerable amount of money home. One night after work she was standing at a bus stop waiting for the bus. It was winter and already dark. She had that day's shop takings in her handbag.

In the gloom coming towards her, she saw a youth. From his energy she saw that he intended to mug her. Did she tense up and grab the bag tight as most people would do? No. She relaxed as much as she could and put white light around herself. She heard the youth's footsteps running towards her, getting nearer and nearer. Suddenly they stopped and she opened her eyes. She saw the young man's hand stretched out to grab her bag but it couldn't get through the white light. On his face was a look of indescribable horror. Then he turned and ran away as fast as he could.

When she relaxed and visualised the white light round herself, she allowed angelic protection to come to her assistance.

When I told a lawyer this story, he smiled and told me of his experience of the power of white light. He said that it was the first time he invoked it but he firmly believed it saved his life.

He was being driven by some friends on the continent. They were driving extremely fast and he felt the presence of imminent danger. He had a choice, either to go into abject terror or to trust the spiritual forces available to him. He decided to relax and protect himself with white light. Once he had done this, he sat back and knew he would be all right.

As they raced at breakneck speed down the motorway, the car in front of them had a puncture. It went all over the road but by some miracle — or by the protective power of the angels of light — missed them and their car was completely untouched.

Do we need to have trust in white light for it to work? Like everything else it follows the spiritual laws of the Universe. To the exact extent that we relax and trust, the angels can come close and help us.

I firmly believe that one person's faith is stronger than the accumulated doubt of many.

At a workshop a participant, Celia, told me that she was taken by a friend to a healing course. They were a little late but trusted that there would be a parking space for them. They toured round and round but couldn't find one. Finally they came across a space in a line of cars illegally parked. Celia's friend said, "We are doing God's work today. We can safely park here." She got out and put white light round the car.

Celia was most agitated and upset. All morning she worried about the car getting a parking ticket but her friend was not concerned. At lunch time Celia wanted to go back and check that the car had not been clamped or towed away. Her friend was bemused because she knew that the car was protected by white angels but Celia dragged her back.

Every other car in the street had a parking ticket firmly attached to its windscreen. Their car was untouched.

Celia was amazed. When she realised just how much worry she had projected into the parking space, she became aware that the angels of white light were much stronger than her negativity.

Angels are stronger than our doubts and fears.

CHAPTER 18

Angels Answer Our Prayers

Joanna confessed that she had been dreading coming for her appointment to release childhood sexual abuse. Just before her appointment she had this dream.

I am a native American Indian woman. I live with my partner and parents. I really love my partner and we have a very close relationship. We live in a log cabin isolated from the others. One day a civil war soldier who had gone off the rails came to the cabin. He had a big gun and kept shooting. He shot the family and the animals and then turned to me and said, "I'm going to sow my seed in you so you'll never forget me". He raped me again and again and I squeezed myself up so I couldn't become pregnant...

I noticed that she started telling the dream in the present tense. Then as it became painful she disassociated from it by slipping into the past tense.

When Joanna woke from this very vivid dream, she realised it was a past life dream. She felt that all her life she had been waiting for the return of the partner who had been so cruelly killed. She told me that she had always kept men at bay and was still a virgin.

Then Joanna started to cry and said that when she was

three years old, a business associate of her father's, who used to come to the house, frequently touched her genitals. She dare not tell anyone because he had told her that if she said anything he would kill her Mum and Dad.

As soon as she had told her story, angels came towards her. I watched them pulling black snakes out of her heart centre.

They indicated that she must close her eyes and go back into her childhood to the time when she was three. When she regressed to three years old again, knowing that the angels were protecting her, she was able to face the abusive man. When he threatened to kill her parents, the child laughed and called him a coward.

I directed her to bring her father into the room and tell him what had happened. She did so and was totally amazed at what unfolded as she watched. "Dad punched him", she exclaimed. "I didn't think he had it in him." For the first time in her life, she realised that he could and would defend her.

Her father turned to her and said, "You deserve to be treated with love and respect." She became aware that she had never believed she deserved to be treated well. Her Dad continued, "Now I understand why you didn't trust me. I've always felt the barrier between us."

Joanna exclaimed, "I thought that if he could let someone do that to me, then he could do it as well. Now I realise that he didn't know what was happening and that if he had known he would have defended me. My anger has gone. I didn't realise it wasn't his fault. I really feel I love him."

Then her mother came into the scene and immediately started to attack the abuser with ferocity and force. Suddenly Joanna exclaimed, "She knew. She knew something was going on."

I pointed out that sometimes we know subliminally but that's not the same as having concrete information. Joanna agreed, "Yes, she knew subliminally and she told Dad to get his business out of the house." She realised that must have been hard for her unassertive mother to do this and that she had acted on her instincts and done her very best to try to help her child.

Joanna sighed and said that her anger towards her mother had all gone.

The angels started to dissolve the dark cloud of anger which had been released. As they did so, we could see that under cover of the darkness Joanna was chained to her parents — with big heavy black chains. We watched while the angels cut the chains and dissolved them in the light.

Then I was shown that Joanna's insides had been sewn up so that she could not have sex. An angel pulled out all the threads. Suddenly there were hundreds of angels standing around them singing.

Joanna's face was bright red and her eyes shining when she opened them. "I've been healed. I know I have," she said.

She told me then that she had never been able to get away from her parents although she had tried all sorts of things. Now she realised that the childhood abuse had chained her literally to the scene.

She said that before she came for the session she had prayed that the angels would come in and help her. Our prayers are always answered.

I spoke to Joanna a couple of months later. She said to me, "I feel whole for the first time in my life. I feel that I am no longer looking for love, support and protection outside myself." Then she added. "Before, I knew that intellectually, but now I feel it inside. I've got more confidence and self-worth. I can't think of a better way to put it than that I feel whole."

Thank you angels.

CHAPTER 19

Angels of Love

Sometimes we can be very caring and spiritual people and yet have illnesses or disabilities for which we can find no cause in this life. Larry was one such young man. He worked only intermittently because of a bad back and permanent tiredness.

When I directed his unconscious mind to take him to the source of his problem, he found himself as a newborn baby full of hate.

He must have carried unresolved hatred in his soul which he had brought into this life. Naturally it affected his relationships, his life's journey and his health.

With a visualisation I helped him open his heart centre and held the energy while angels came into the room and in their infinite love and mercy pulled the dark hatred from his heart. Then they filled his heart with light and peace.

He phoned a few days later to say how incredibly different he felt.

We are so afraid of our darkness that we often deny it. A young lady, Pauline, who had done a great deal of personal growth work came to me with a jealousy problem. Of course, a problem with jealousy is always a problem about not feeling good enough.

I asked if she had sought the past life cause of her jealousy and she said she had experienced several regressions. They had all helped to scrape away some of the problem but none had cleared out the darkness.

I had a feeling that this session might be different because a very beautiful angel had come into the room with her and was making itself visible to me. It was hovering above her with its hands in a praying position and I knew that we must ask for grace to release the blockage.

The angel showed me a door in the young lady's mind, fastened with rusty bolts and a similar one in her heart! I was being shown that the darkness which caused her to feel so bad was locked into her heart and mind. She felt so unworthy that she constantly expected her partners to find someone else better.

When I regressed her she discovered that in another life she had been a light soul born to a mother who was a black witch, filled with hatred. Instead of bringing light into this family of darkness, which had been her intention when she chose that challenging life, she allowed the terrible darkness to fill her. She felt consumed with black rage and hatred of all people and life itself.

Her beautiful angel, radiating gold, deep blue and pink, now put its hands into her chest and round her heart. Pauline and I could both see the blackness, like an octopus clinging to her heart, with its huge tentacles spreading through her body.

I expected the angel to take the octopus and dissolve it in the light. Instead it very gently and lovingly lifted it from Pauline's heart, stroked it and took it away for healing. Then the angel came back and lifted Pauline's heart out of her body and took it for cleansing and purification in a beautiful waterfall.

When her heart was returned to her body, I presumed that would be the end but no. The angel brought back the octopus transformed through divine love into something pink. Pauline saw a rose quartz crystal. We put the crystal into her heart and by now she was glowing.

When she opened her eyes at the end of the session she said she felt that something really deep had taken place. She knew there had been a major change within her.

Angels, with their infinite love and compassion, are waiting to help us.

CHAPTER 20

Earth Angels

There have always been reports of people arriving from nowhere and helping others, then disappearing. Many believe these to be angels, using human guise.

A friend of mine wrote me this note about his conversation at a party with a lovely, really sprightly lady in her 70s. "She told me that she was at Victoria coach station looking for a coach to Gatwick, and realised that she would not make it. She stood with her baggage and prayed for help, and a little black man appeared by her and said that he could help her. He was sent by God, he said, and took her and her baggage to the BA check in at the railway station, and put her on the train in plenty of time to catch her flight. She is convinced that he was an angel.

I was told the following story by a friend, who has had a very special and charmed life. She believes that an Earth angel helped her even before she was born. At that time her mother was eight months pregnant with her and certainly was not anticipating her imminent arrival.

The family lived in a small village in the country where everyone knew everyone else. Her mother was scrubbing the front door step when a stranger appeared at the front gate and told her to send for her husband and doctor and to go and lie down immediately. The baby was about to be born.

Such was the command in the stranger's voice that her mother unquestioningly did what she was told. Her husband came home quickly. The doctor arrived and the baby was born within the hour.

Upon enquiry round the village, no one had seen a stranger that morning.

Earth angels appear
and then disappear when their task is accomplished.

Recently I was sent a letter with this story of extraordinary help from Patricia O'Flaherty.

In 1980, in October, we moved as a family to Norway in connection with my (now ex) husband's work. The children were eight and six respectively. It was a tremendous upheaval. We'd had three weeks notice. I'd had to give up my job, pack up the house, organise 1001 things and had had little sleep and a lot of anxiety. We arrived in Oslo by car after a twenty-four hour ferry journey and a long drive through Sweden and southern Norway and finally booked into the Grand Hotel where we were to stay for two weeks whilst we found accommodation.

The first day or two we collapsed and slept and ventured out on short trips as a family in the car. But on Monday morning my husband went to work and the children were feeling perky and energetic. I felt awful: sick, muzzy headed, shaky and exhausted but after lunch we decided to have a little wander to explore the city.

We set off. I hadn't intended to go far but somehow we seemed to get further and further away from the shops. The day got darker and darker. Cars were driving with their lights on. It was bitterly cold and suddenly we were lost somewhere under a motorway flyover.

I felt panic stricken. The children were tired. There was no-one about and I thought I might faint. I was feeling so peculiar. I remember asking for help from the bottom of my heart. There was no way I could get out of this pickle myself.

Suddenly, a tall, fair man in a raincoat appeared from somewhere. I didn't notice where. He understood English perfectly and smilingly, kindly, started to escort us. The rest of the journey is like a dream that one has. Suffice to say, I "came to" at the kiosk on the corner by the Grand Hotel.

I have no explanation for what happened but am convinced it was an angel helping us home.

If a child is whining and whingeing without really trying, we tend to ignore him. But if the child is in genuine trouble or despair, we naturally rush to his assistance. We are God's children and I believe that when we are in real need, God sends a person or an angel to help to us.

This has happened to me in many ways big and small since my very first cry for help was answered by the being of light. I think I was such a long way down the pit of despondency that I needed a lot of help to get out of it.

A year or so after that first experience, I was still feeling very frightened and alone. I went to a lecture. I sat at the front of the hall and have to confess I couldn't concentrate on the talk, as I was so entrenched in my own survival fears. After the lecture a stranger came up to me from the back of the hall. He apologised for tuning into my thoughts during the talk but he was to tell me that everything would be all right. I must not worry for I was being guided and protected.

On a second occasion a stranger came up to me in the street and gave me an almost identical message. I do not imagine these were angels but I expect they were prompted by higher beings to give me these messages of hope.

On a third occasion I was feeling very low . Something made me look up into the sky. I saw huge upturned hands filling the sky as if to say. We will hold you. I could hardly believe what I saw but it encouraged me greatly.

Earth angels come to help, encourage and support us.

CHAPTER 21

Practical Angels

There are myriads of angels ready and willing to help human souls. We only have to ask and they are there bringing us what we need.

Lots of people know about the angel of parking spaces. When we ask for an angel of parking spaces and tell him where we want our space prepared, he will do his utmost to clear that space for us. It is the same with the angel of traffic lights. Ask your angel to turn them green as quickly as possible to facilitate your journey.

A friend visiting from Canada told me that he always asked his driving angel to protect him from speed traps and cameras when in the car. He said it worked amazingly. He would do nothing consciously but would find that his speed had slowed down and he would hear of others being fined at that spot on that day.

I have always used white light to protect my car, that is, until the angels made their presence known. While I believe that it is the same angelic energy, it feels much more personal to have an angel guarding my car or my home.

A lady on a workshop told me that she always asked an angel to watch over her car and although she left it in some very unsafe areas, it was never touched. Then over time she got to feel that the angel no longer wanted to do that job. She didn't know why. It was just an impression she had, so one day she released the angel from the work of protecting her car. Next day it was broken into.

Now I don't understand why she should have received such an impression. Maybe she needed to experience a robbery which could not take place while an angel was on guard?

Another lady on a workshop had us all in fits of laughter when she shared how she always invited an angel to help with the housework. Before she started to vacuum the house she would invite in her vacuuming angel and the chore would be done in half the normal time, easily and lightly. When the washing machine broke down and there was a huge pile of washing to be done by hand, she said, "It was no trouble. I asked the washing angel to help and the whole lot was done in two hours and I felt wonderful." It seems they give us energy as they help.

Angels are so full of delight. They help us lightly with shopping, typing, accounts, literally anything we want. Isn't it wonderful to think that when we are struggling to balance the books, there is an accounting angel hovering above the computer waiting to make it all easy. When we are agonising over which present to buy, there is a shopping angel longing to point us towards the perfect gift!

We do make life difficult for ourselves... and there are all those angels just waiting to smooth the way for us as long as our intentions are pure.

As well as guardian angels, there are angels of mercy, truth, love, compassion, humility, peace and every conceivable quality. When we live at higher levels of consciousness we pray for qualities rather than things.

Spiritual Law says that whatever we focus on increases. So when we focus on a quality such as love or peace an angel helps bring more of this higher quality into our lives.

Of course, the same is true of the lower qualities. If we focus on fear, greed, lust or any negative quality the dark forces will direct more of these feelings and events into our lives.

However angels bring hope. They try to inspire and comfort us in times of trouble. Sometimes we feel too down to feel their presence even though they are trying to lift us. Then, if it is karmically permitted, they will inspire someone to lighten us.

My son, Justin, tells a delightful story about an incident he witnessed on the underground. The train was fairly crowded and there was one woman in the compartment who was glowering at everyone. She looked so unhappy and forbidding that the atmosphere in the compartment was getting heavier and heavier. When the train stopped, a young man got in. He sat down and pulled two very long thin balloons out of his pocket, one red and one green. Everyone was watching as he blew them up. He proceeded to twist the balloons together until he had fashioned a red rose. At the next station he got up and presented the rose to the glowering lady. Then he jumped off the train. Suddenly she was beaming from ear to ear as she held the balloon rose. Justin found himself smiling broadly as he watched. He looked round and everyone was grinning and laughing with pleasure.

Angels bring light
to the heaviest tasks and darkest situations.

CHAPTER 22

Angels Help a Marriage

Serena was a young and attractive married woman with small children. Her looks belied an inner turmoil. She was so angry with her husband, who could not support her financially and emotionally, that she had refused to have sex with him for several years. She was contemplating living with him in this celibate way until the children were older because she could not bear the thought of him touching her.

I talked with her for some time helping her to become more aware of her patterns and then she agreed to relax and invite the angels in to help her.

As soon as the angels came closer, they moved to her heart and showed me that her heart was very bruised emotionally. They stroked and soothed her bruised heart until it was mended.

Then they moved down to her solar plexus. It was like a dusty cellar full of old memories and they worked hard to clear out all the rubbish and take it to the light where it was dissolved. When they had cleared out and cleansed and blessed her solar plexus I asked her to imagine her husband in front of her.

"Oh, I'm surrounded in black and he's all black and red," she said. Black and red together are the colours of imminent explosion. He was clearly at the end of his tether.

The angels took a long time gently washing away all the

dark angry energy around both of them and dissolved the cords which entangled them.

When they had done this, Serena said to me, "We are holding hands and supporting each other and we share our body fluids." I was quite surprised at this. However, I merely asked the angels if they would continue to bring both of them together.

She returned for another appointment two weeks later and I was delighted at the vibrant and glowing woman who walked in. She said that after the help from the angels she had gone home feeling totally different. She and her husband had a night of passion.

Next day she felt a bit angry and scared but that passed and now they were loving and close to each other and making love again. She said, "I can now clearly see how I can make things work not what he has to do. I am clear about where I am going with my work and realise we can now be joint providers. For the first time I feel quite comfortable with that."

She added that a friend, who was staying with them, had stayed with them four months earlier and was astonished at the difference in their relationship — she could hardly believe it.

When we allow them to,
angels will do their best
to bring two partners in a marriage together.

CHAPTER 23

Angels and the Nature Kingdoms

Angels are guardians of the natural world. They lovingly assist humans and the nature kingdoms to evolve. They direct the elementals who tend nature. These are the fairies, elves, gnomes, sylphs, salamanders, pixies and fauns among others.

Where these elementals live in close proximity to humans, they are affected by our emotions, attaching to whatever energy is available. They link as easily to our dark thoughts as to our positive energy, expanding either. Anyone working with crystals will be aware that the elemental within the crystal will magnify negative energy as well as positive healing energy. So elementals can be destructive or constructive.

It works like this. Salamanders, the fire elementals, help fires to burn. When we are gathered round a cheerful blaze, the salamanders are merrily at work. If humans are angry and out of harmony, salamanders can respond by creating havoc with fire. If a house or neighbourhood burns down, the salamanders are sparked by the — often suppressed — chaotic emotions of the people who live there.

Fire is also a cleanser. When people are cremated, the salamanders help with the release of old family patterns, negative habits and thought forms which might otherwise attach to vulnerable members of the family who are still alive.

I was told this delightful story by Pamela Russell of Evesham who used to own a soft furnishings shop, which was in a small cottage in an old listed building. Before she bought it an elderly lady had lived there for many years until she had gone into a home and eventually died. The old lady had been very fond of her home and her presence was frequently felt. She was also quite mischievous. Pamela would leave her favourite thimble with her work and it would sometimes just disappear. Everyone would hunt for it. Then they would firmly tell the spirit of the old lady to return it and next morning it would be sitting in the middle of the table! Apparently this only happened when a new employee came to work there. It was as if the old lady's ghost wanted to know who had come into her home and be acknowledged by that person. So she made her presence felt until she received attention and acknowledgement by her tricks. Once she had accepted and been accepted by the newcomer, she stopped hiding the thimble.

Whenever the thimble vanished or they sensed her presence, there would be a lovely smell of flowers in the room. They could smell stocks, lilies of the valley and sweet peas. The old lady's daughter-in-law told Pamela that, when she was alive, her mother-in-law used to make bouquets of flowers and wreaths from old fashioned scented garden flowers.

Then one day there was a fire in the shop. After the mess was cleared up and the shop repainted the old lady never came back. I suspect the fire elementals cleansed the old memories away, so that the old lady was no longer attached to her home and decided to move on to where she should be.

The air spirits are sylphs. They smile in the gentle breeze of summer or they can be whipped up into frenzied tornados or hurricanes. The sylphs link into our suppressed anger and express it for us.

When someone says they are going to brave the elements, they literally mean they are going to brave the elemental energy of air, water, fire or earth which is being released.

Fairies take care of flowers. Where we garden organically and they feel safe and loved, fairies will help flowers and vegetables to grow. I know many people who have seen fairies or have them living in their gardens or even window boxes.

However, I have only ever once seen a fairy myself and that was at the Findhorn Foundation, the huge spiritual community in Scotland. They are renowned for their wonderful produce, which is grown in attunement with nature. There, the veil between the worlds is very thin.

Seeing that fairy was an experience I shall never forget. I was listening to a talk. In the middle of the room was a bowl of catmint flowers with a candle in the centre of it. (Catmint leaves are silver but the flowers are a beautiful mauvish blue.) To my surprise and delight I saw a brilliant light, the exact colour of the flowers, hovering above the vase. It was a fairy, looking exactly like Tinkerbell from the Peter Pan books I loved in childhood, only shimmering, shining and luminous in a way I would not have expected. I watched it move above and around the flowers. Even when I looked away and back again it was still there. It was much more enthralling than the lecture but eventually I had to focus on the work again and the beautiful fairy disappeared from my sight.

There are undines, who are water sprites, and mermaids, who tend plants under the sea. The earth elementals are the gnomes, who work with stones, minerals and jewels.

These spirits are only made up of one element, unlike humans who consist of all four: air, water, fire and earth. Any of the elementals can be mischievous. It behoves us to treat them with firm respect.

There are two parallel streams of evolution. One is the angelic stream. The young ones of this stream are the elementals, who eventually evolve into angels through the various orders, overseen by the Lords of Karma and, ultimately, by Source.

The other evolutionary thread is that along which animals and humans evolve. Above us in the hierarchy are the spirit guides under the direction of the Ascended Masters, again answerable to Source.

When we honour the natural world, we help the angels and according to spiritual law we in turn receive help.

CHAPTER 24

Interdimensional Portals

All the mountains, rivers, rocks and trees have their own angel to guard them and, of course, to direct the elementals who work within them.

When we have a sense of the power of a mountain or of a waterfall, we are in tune with the angel who is guarding that place.

There are power spots on planet Earth to which people are drawn because they feel peaceful or relaxed when they are there. Usually these are places of great natural beauty which induce a sense of wonder and awe.

I had an unexpected experience at Avebury, which is the heart chakra of the planet and one of the power spots in England. While I was meditating at one of the standing stones, I sent out a silent prayer to see the angel of Avebury who guarded the power spot. Immediately I had the impression of an immense force about the size of three skyscrapers — absolutely vast. It surrounded me and was not the warm gentle feeling of the angels I had met up to that time. It was a fierce, protective and powerful force — a positive force for those of good intent but certainly not one to be tampered with. I felt as if it were pushing me into the stone. Whew! I realised then something of the might of the angels.

Some of these power spots are interdimensional portals through which humans and beings in other dimensions can communicate more easily. Being at one of these gateways leaves us open to impressions, visions, intuitive flashes and any form of spiritual or psychic message.

A great many of the interdimensional portals are one-way; in other words, the higher beings can come through the vortex to communicate with us. A few of them are two-way and through these we can receive universal messages as well as transmit out into the Universe. Stonehenge in England is one such two-way communication centre, which has been re-opened at this moment in time. The most powerful interdimensional portal on planet Earth is Machu Picchu in Peru.

The only entry aliens have to our planet is through these portals. Even angels find it easier to use these open gateways to access our planet. However, if we do not protect these, our precious entry points, dark angels and negative aliens can come through. And we have stopped protecting and putting light into these powerful interdimensional portals.

Originally these portals were most sacred and holy places, looked after with ceremony and love by specially trained initiates. Now we neglect them.

I recently went to Machu Picchu with friends. We had terrible nightmares, which we were told on return, were the dark forces attacking us. Nevertheless, we were informed that the area drank in the light we took with us like parched earth responding to gentle rain. Certainly meditating and ohm-ing at Macchu Pichu was the highlight of the trip for me. I felt the energy being drawn up from me.

When humans of high intention and spiritual focus visit or think about Stonehenge, Macchu Pichu and other portals their light automatically helps to protect these important gateways. We can also pour love and light energy out into the Universe through these portals.

All crop circles are formed and placed by the turquoise angels of communication. Crop circles are symbols. Whenever we see pictures of them in a newspaper or flashed onto a TV screen, the symbols are keys which unlock universal information within our minds. We do not need consciously to decode each symbol for the messages work subliminally.

In 1996 a huge crop circle was formed opposite Stonehenge. I was told that it was placed there to increase the energy of the interdimensional portal. The coded message of the symbol was about intergalactic travel. It invited people to go through the portal in their dream states and travel intergalactically, so that they could learn about the vastness of the Universe. This would expand their consciousness.

Whenever people sit in a crop circle they connect with the angels.

Many of the dark forces, or evil forces as some people prefer to call them, have been able to draw near over the last few thousand years because of our neglect of the sacred protection rituals and the sheer amount of negativity and fear that humans on planet Earth have sent out. Our darkness feeds the consciousness of the dark angels and keeps them alive and active around us. However, unless we send out our own fear and negativity, they cannot influence us in any way.

The many light beings and angels, who so much want to approach and work with us, need a love vibration from us in order to be able to come closer. The love energy we radiate also provides nourishment and food for the angels. They need to be loved and nourished as much as we do. When we project love, gratitude and other high vibrations out through the portals into the Universe, we send an invitation for the higher consciousness to come to us.

It is imperative at this time of shift of consciousness on planet Earth that we send light along the ley lines that connect us to the other planets and galaxies so that Earth can be realigned and take its rightful place in the Universe. This we can more effectively do through the interdimensional portals.

Of course, it helps to send out as much love, light and higher energy as we can at all times. However, when we project our call for more love and help through the portals, it goes further out into the Universe where highly evolved light beings can respond.

When we ask the angels to help they will direct our beams of love and light to the best possible place.

Light means spiritual knowledge and information.
Darkness is absence of light.
Being in the dark literally means
having no spiritual knowing.
Power spots are good places to visit
if we wish to open up more quickly to the light.

CHAPTER 25

The Angelic Hierarchy

It is widely believed that angels were created by Source before humans were added to the universal scheme of things. When humans were created some of the lower orders of angels were delegated to look after us.

There are diverse opinions about the various orders of angels. It is generally considered that they are made up of three hierarchies with three levels in each.

The first and highest sphere are the Seraphim, Cherubim and Thrones.

The second sphere are the Dominions, Virtues and Powers

The third and lowest sphere are the Principalities, Archangels and Angels.

The highest order of the angelic hierarchy are the Seraphim, whose essence is pure love. They are the heavenly hosts who constantly sing the praises of the Creator, thus maintaining the vibration of creation. They direct the divine energy as it emanates from Source. Only these highest voltage beings can accept such a level of God-force.

The Cherubim, the angels of wisdom, spread this unimaginable light. They are guardians of the stars and the celestial heavens. We are told that after Adam and Eve's fall from grace, God set one of the Cherubim before the Garden of Eden to guard the way to the Tree of Life.

The Thrones look after and guard the planets. The angel in charge of our planet, Earth, is therefore a Throne. Ezekiel, the Hebrew prophet describes them as flaming torches or burning coals of fire. They are often depicted as having many eyes, or even wheels.

This trio, the Seraphim, Cherubim and Thrones, receives direct illumination from Source and they transform the light in order to transmit it at a level that can be accepted by lower orders in the Universe.

The Dominions are celestial prefects, overseeing those in the angelic realms who are at a lower level than they are. They are channels of mercy and although they rarely connect with humans they help to smooth the passage between the spiritual and the material.

The Virtues send out vast beams of light in a form accessible to us humans. These are the angels who make miracles happen. When groups raise their consciousness and tune into angel energy, they access the pool of information the Virtues radiate. These awarenesses will facilitate the rise in consciousness for the New Age.

We may never have heard of the Powers but most of us have heard of the angels of birth and death. The angel of birth, who lovingly enfolds us at our moment of birth, is a Power as is the angel who joyously helps us with our transition from our human body into the light body at death. They will help and guide humans if they are lost in the astral planes after leaving their bodies. The Lords of Karma, who are in overall charge of the karmic records, are Powers. They guard the conscience of humankind. There are also Lords of Group Karma, National Karma, World Karma and Universal Karma.

Principalities look after and protect cities, nations, multinational corporations and any very large structure of people. Like all the angelic hosts they work throughout the Universe, and Earth is a very small part of their domain.

Then there are the Archangels, who lead bands of angels. They oversee vast projects for the light. While there are millions of Archangels throughout the Universe, those most closely connected with Earth are Michael, Gabriel, Raphael and Uriel. Of these only three are mentioned in the Bible. These are Gabriel, whose name means 'Hero of God' or 'God is my Strength', Raphael meaning 'God has Healed' and Michael meaning 'One who is like God'. Archangel Michael is often seen as a warrior angel and is also the guardian of the lonely traveller.

Uriel's name means 'Fire of God' and it is Archangel Uriel who gave the Kabbalah, the Hebrew mystic tradition, to humanity.

The Archangels have retreat locations in the etheric around planet Earth. We can ask at night before we go to sleep to be taken to one of these retreats for purification and any help we may need.

Archangel Michael's retreat is at Banff in Alberta, Canada, while Archangel Uriel is in the Tatra Mountains, south of Cracow, Poland and Archangel Raphael's retreat is in Fatima, Portugal. Archangel Gabriel's retreat is at Mount Shasta, California.

We can ask to go to Archangel Jophiel's retreat south of the Great Wall near Lanchow, North Central China. His name means 'Beauty of God'. Chamuel, 'He who sees God' is at St Louis, Missouri, USA. Archangel Zadkiel, 'Righteousness of God', is in Cuba.

The Iranian Archangel Voku Monak revealed God's message to Zoroaster 2500 years ago. The Zoroastrians said that six Archangels guarded the presence of Ahura Mazda, known as the Lord of Light or the Wise Lord. These Archangels personified Good Wind, Excellent Truth, Wished for Kingdom, Devotion, Wholesomeness and Non Death. It is said that Ahura Mazda flies in a disc of light and this is how he is depicted in ancient carvings.

In Islam the angelic hierarchy is headed by Archangel Gabriel, who dictated the Koran to Mohammed. The Sufis of the Islamic mystery schools are strongly connected to angels.

Another Archangel, Moroni, facilitated the discovery of divinely inscribed golden tablets which became the Book of Mormon, and established the Mormon religion.

It is from the lowest rank, that of angels, that the guardians who work with humans are selected. While they guard us from birth, they are also available to guide us and help us in many ways, if only we will ask. They can smooth our path, heal through us, inspire us, fill us with higher energies and work with us to create a harmonious life and spread the light.

Angels are our guardians on Earth. We each have a personal guardian angel, who is a recording angel. In other words our guardian angel notes our thoughts and deeds and keeps our individual akashic records up to date. These are overseen by Lords of Karma.

Angels serve at different levels throughout the Universe.

CHAPTER 26

Angels from the Bible

Angels appear throughout the Christian Bible, serving a variety of functions.

Messenger Angels

The best known of these are the messengers who appeared at the time of the birth of Jesus, the Christ. Before Mary's wedding to Joseph, an angel appeared to Mary and told her that she would bear a son, who would be the son of God.

It seems that Joseph was not receptive to angels when he was fully awake, so one came to him in a dream to inform him that indeed Mary's child would be the Messiah. Then an angel appeared to shepherds to tell them that their saviour had been born and they were surrounded by a whole host of angels singing, "Glory be to God in heaven and on Earth be peace."

The wise men followed a shining star to the stable where Jesus was born. They had been asked by Herod to tell him where the child was but angels warned them not to go back to Herod and they left the country by a different route. When Herod in a rage ordered the death of every boy under the age of two, again an angel warned Joseph in a dream, so that he and Mary fled with their son to Egypt.

On another occasion two shining white angels appeared to the disciples to give them the message that Jesus had been taken from Earth to Heaven — and in the same way He would return from Heaven to Earth.

People were receptive to angels in the early Christian times just as they are becoming again. Cornelius was a Roman centurion in Caesarea. He was a good man, married to a Jewish wife. One day he heard an angel call his name and tell him to go to Simon's house, where Peter lodged.

In the meantime Peter was praying on a rooftop when he was shown a vision. He saw an enormous sheet tied at the corners and filled with all kinds of animals including pigs, goats, lambs, wolves and chickens. A voice told him to choose and eat.

Peter was a Jew and unable to eat meat not killed according to Jewish law. He said so. The angelic voice replied, "What God calls fit, let no mortal call unfit." He saw the vision twice more and heard the same words. As he left the roof, Roman soldiers were hammering on the door. The angel told him to go with them and fear nothing for they had been sent by Jesus.

The soldiers took him to Cornelius who implored him to teach and baptise all the people he had gathered. Many of the elders were horrified. They thought that non-Jews should not become Christians. Peter, however, remembered what the angel said, "What God calls fit, let no mortal think unfit."

He reminded the elders that God accepts everyone. A rushing wind was heard, which was presumably the sound of angels' wings, and tongues of fire flickered above the crowd.

Rescuing Angels

Angels do save humans from danger. Daniel was placed in a den of hungry lions where he would starve to death even if the lions did not kill him. However, an angel was sent to a farmer called Habbakuk, who had just packed a basket of food. The angel carried him with the basket to the lions' den where the terrified farmer gave the food to Daniel.

Presumably the angel did not need to save Daniel from the lions or else he would have done so. In ancient times initiates were trained in the temples to hold their thoughts totally steady, without fear, so that they could control lions, snakes or any other creature. In some lifetime Daniel must have had this training.

When Nebuchadnezzar was king in Babylon three Jews called Shadrach, Meshach and Abednego refused to worship the huge statue he had built. They were told that they would be chained and thrown into the fiery furnace if they did not worship the idol.

When they still refused, they were indeed thrown into the fiery furnace. Instead of the usual screams when people burnt to death, the watching dignitaries heard only singing. A white-faced Nebuchadnezzar pointed at the flames and said he could see the three men and an angel walking in the flames and singing.

The king ordered them out and they stepped from the flames. The fire had melted the chains which had fallen away. Their bodies, hair and clothes were untouched and instead of the smell of singed flesh, only the perfume of flowers could be smelt.

Angels of Destruction

There are also angels of destruction. The old and bad is destroyed to make way for the new and good. This is also the task of Shiva, the Hindu God (or angel).

There was a city called Sodom in which all sorts of lust and licentiousness were practised. Abraham pleaded with God not to destroy the honest and good people as well as the debauched ones. God promised that if ten honest people could be found, all the people of the city would be spared. However, only one honest person, a man called Lot, could be discovered living in Sodom and God's angels destroyed the city.

Now it may well be that a physical earthquake caused the destruction of the area but the angels oversee all of nature, including earthquakes.

Helping Angels

Even in biblical times Archangels came down to Earth disguised as human beings to help the good in response to their prayers. Tobit was one such good man who helped the poor and disadvantaged. One night he was blinded and could no longer work, so he and his family became very poor. He prayed for help.

At the same time in another town a good woman, called Sarah was having an unbelievably difficult time. She had married seven times and each time her new groom was found dead in the morning! No one knew why this should be so but the devil had killed them. So poor Sarah still had to live with her parents and no one wanted to marry her. She prayed for help.

Tobit and Sarah's prayers reached God and Archangel Raphael was despatched to Earth in human disguise to help them. God reminded Tobit that he was owed silver by his cousin, who was Sarah's father. The money would greatly help his financial situation. God also impressed upon Tobit that his son Tobias could travel to the distant town to fetch it.

Archangel Raphael took on the role of a camel driver, who was hired by Tobias to take him across the desert to fetch the silver. On the way Tobias went to wash in a wide river. A glittering fish jumped out of the water and Raphael told him to keep its liver, heart and gall bladder in little sealed pots.

When they eventually reached Sarah's family, her father not only handed over the silver but asked Tobias to marry his daughter. Tobias did not want to be the eighth dead husband, so he asked his servant for advice. Raphael suggested he marry the girl and told him to use specific psychic protection — burning the heart and liver of the fish.

The marriage took place. Throughout the wedding night

Tobias fed the fire and burnt the heart and liver of the fish as suggested by Raphael. When the devil entered, he was repelled by the smell of the burning offal so that he could not harm Tobias. Then Raphael chased and overcame him.

The young couple journeyed back across the desert to Tobias's family home. Before he met his father again, Raphael told Tobias how to heal the old man's blindness using the gall of the fish. When the father's sight returned, he recognised Raphael as an angel. Raphael then disappeared.

Angels constantly do God's bidding.

CHAPTER 27

Angels in Churches

Most of us have gone into a church or cathedral sometime and felt a sense of peace and stillness. This is because angels have contained the energy in the sacred space for centuries.

The angel of a church can also be extremely protective. A friend of mine decided to have a very quiet, meditative Christmas. She went to a church to sit alone. As she entered she felt the presence of a golden angel filling the church. She told me she had a sense of how strong, how powerful and how fierce it was. This was not a frightening experience. Rather it was reassuring to know that the angel was so immense and so protective. She felt safe and enfolded within its energy. It is the only experience of this kind she has ever had.

People very often have spiritual and angelic experiences when they are out in nature. This is because the angels do not judge or criticise us. Surrounded only by the angels of trees, rocks, mountains and streams, who accept us as we are, we are safe. When we feel this security we can relax our guard. This is when we open up to the higher dimensions.

In a church, or to be more accurate, in a building used for spiritual purposes, there can be a similar feeling of safety. If the congregations are spiritual enough to be non-judgemental and accepting of all, then the place is steeped in the peace that allows us to still our minds and open our hearts.

There is much noise, disharmony, excitement and violence in the world. We can never find the path to Source when we are constantly busy and distracted. Churches and temples are usually quiet, peaceful places where we can centre ourselves.

In order to connect to our intuition we must become still . To find our wisdom we must listen in silence. When we sit daily in inner peace, quiet and stillness our way forward is revealed and smoothed. It is when we connect to Source that we find true refreshment for our spirit. It is in the stillness of our hearts and minds that our emptiness can be filled with love.

When we become calm, centred and still we radiate such wonderful waves of peace around us that people want to bathe in our sea of harmony.

The angels of nature, of churches and of truly spiritual places help to calm and soothe troubled minds and hearts. They provide a calm safe place where this connection can be made.

Jeanne Slade, whose story I told in Chapter 7, recently went to the Domo in Florence. She stood in a group of people at the back of the Domo and relaxed in the energy. She felt nothing on the left of the cathedral. Then she had a terrific feeling inside her and her eyes were drawn to a space on the right. There was such an enormous loving presence emanating from the right that she found herself riveted. It reached all the way up to the ceiling and filled the space. Despite her frustration that she could not see this huge angel, she could feel the loving angel presence so strongly that her heart felt as if it was being opened and expanded.

*When you relax into the love of angels,
your heart will be opened.*

CHAPTER 28

Dark Angels

We have been fed with stories of dark angels or fallen angels who have rebelled against God and become evil and vengeful. They are known as Lucifer, Satan, Mephistopheles, Samael or Beelzebub amongst other names. All religions refer to dark angels or gods who tempt or destroy. I believe it is only on planet Earth, the plane of free choice and duality, that these dark forces could gain credence.

In Isaiah God says, "I form the Light and create Darkness." The Creator was always considered to be the source of creation and destruction. It was only two hundred years before the birth of Christ that a belief evolved in a separate force for evil which opposed God.

Source is omnipotent, is light. God is not in competition with evil or the devil, rather He allows them to serve His purpose.

The popular legend is that Lucifer, a Seraph, Bearer of the Light, and beloved of God, challenged Him for his throne. God cast the rebel into the abyss and one-third of the angel host defected from the light with him, becoming dark angels who tempt people into evil, lustful ways.

Ultimately all angels serve Source. It is not possible for Archangels to defect. Angels and Archangels do not rebel against the Creator. What they do is offer their services to God, in this case to test and challenge those on planet Earth.

Earth is unique in that Source decided to set up a free will experiment here. What greater way for beings to grow and experience than to have choice?

The reason for the experiment was this. A state of perfection is not a state of growth. In order to expand, there must be a challenge. There is no yin without yang, no negative without positive, no feminine without masculine. So Earth was designated as a plane of choice where beings could learn to balance the material and spiritual. By experiencing both polarities the consciousness of the beings incarnating here would expand and would enrich Source when they returned Home.

When Source set up this free will zone, nothing less than a great Archangel was needed to oversee the divine project. I believe Archangel Lucifer volunteered to lead this experiment in free choice. We are repeatedly told that Lucifer will one day be reinstated to his original place. This will be when all on planet Earth raise their consciousness and integrate their shadow side. Then his task will be done.

In order to participate in the free will experiment, Lucifer and his volunteers also agreed to be shut off from their connection with Source. Once in the dark Lucifer swung to the negative pole and used his enormous power for evil and temptation.

The Creator decreed that all who incarnate here are free to choose their thoughts and actions. Although the spark of divinity remains within us, the memory of our divine heritage was closed down. So on Earth we have total liberty to think negative or positive thoughts, do bad or good deeds. Our growth depends on our personal choice. Furthermore whatever we think, do or believe is mirrored back to us in our lives. This means that each one of us creates our individual reality. When we change our beliefs, thoughts or acts, the universal energy reflects the changes back to us, so we have a different life.

In other words, on Earth our inner world is reflected by

the outer world. This gives us maximum chances for spiritual growth. We grow by facing the tests presented. Every time we make a choice of right thinking or right deeds, we grow lighter. In planes where there is no free choice, growth is slower.

Darkness, negativity or evil is absence of light or lack of spiritual knowledge. When we are in the dark, we feel separate from Source. It hurts and it is only a hurt being who will harm another.

Disconnection from the light lets in guilt, fear and self-deception. When we forget Source or believe we are alone and separate, we depend on and hold onto people. This means we falsely try to please people or control them to avoid the feeling of aloneness. And so the darkness within us grows.

The forgetting of spiritual truths meant that people made choices to hurt others, to destroy the planet, to focus on material possessions and think dark, angry thoughts. The dark angels fed on this negativity and grew in power.

It is very difficult not to be tainted by negativity while we are in a physical body. Even the most beautiful spirits find it hard to withstand the darkness of our planet. Despite the risk of our light being engulfed by the blanket of darkness in this plane, souls from all over the universe wait to incarnate on planet Earth because of the unique challenges and opportunities it offers.

Those who become very negative or closed to the truth will often continue on that path until they feel so hurting that they cry out for help. The angels of light respond to these cries and help them start on their journey back to Source.

Just as angels of light use their power to help, encourage and free people, the dark angels strive to tempt, to whisper thoughts of anger or destruction and to weaken humans. In the free will zone of planet Earth, the dark angels will do anything to achieve their ends, even impersonate light angels. The greatest protection against the voices of darkness, or temptation, are common sense and discrimination as well as good intention and positivity — and always listening to the still quiet voice of conscience within.

If an angel or any other being appears to us, it is always appropriate to challenge whether they are truly of the light. Suitable wording might be, "In the name of God and all that is holy, are you an angel of light?" Challenge in the same words three times. If the answer is "Yes" each time, then accept them. Under the great Spiritual Laws of the Universe, they must speak truthfully if challenged three times in the name of God.

True angels have a golden quality and radiance. This quality is reflected in their whispers into your mind. If the whispers are of love and harmony, justice and acceptance, then they come from the light angels. A light angel will always leave us feeling warm and peaceful.

Angels of light say, "Follow your heart. This is your higher purpose."

Do light angels have free will? The answer is no. Angels' greatest desire is to serve God — to do the will of the Creator. This limits choice. When we humans too rise in consciousness so that our only desire is to follow the will of Source, we will no longer want the freedom to destroy ourselves.

We must always remember that the Divine Intelligence is overseeing the project and light is always more powerful than darkness. No dark force can touch us if we hold onto the light.

During the experiment of free will, humans have overstepped the bounds of what is allowed. We have damaged each other and the planet. This is why there is such a massive rescue mission taking place by angels and other light forces to help us. It is imperative we relax, trust, centre and calm ourselves, so that they can get closer.

Like humans dark angels who have separated themselves from Source for this experiment have freedom to do as they will.

Light angels have no free will
for their only desire is to serve the will of the Creator.

CHAPTER 29

Rescuing Angels

It is during times of danger that people turn to spirit. It takes life-threatening situations for many to remember that there is help available. Perhaps this is why many modern representations of angels are found in military establishments! For instance I understand that there is a beautiful stained glass window at a naval base in California showing Archangel Gabriel.

The appearance of angels at Mons during the First World War have been well reported. It seems that when the British were being defeated by the Germans, angels appeared above the armies and were seen by hundreds of soldiers. According to reports some saw one angel, others a whole host of them. However, it is agreed that the angels intervened to encourage the British army and give it time to disengage.

I am sure that the angels responded to millions of prayers being sent out for both sides by those in the army and those at home. Inevitably the beings of light supported freedom versus aggression and control.

During the Battle of Britain there were aircraft in which the crews had been killed, which continued to fight. Air Chief Marshal Lord Dowding believed that these aircraft were piloted by angels.

As I was writing this a friend told me that her father had

had an angel experience when he was a teenager. He had never mentioned it to her but he had told her mother, who years later had told her.

It happened when he was eighteen and on his first motorbike. The bike skidded in the rain and he was thrown off. By the time the ambulance arrived he was semiconscious. Then as they were about to put him into the ambulance, he heard the soft fluttery sound of wings and felt a wonderful warm safe presence gently lifting him with the ambulance men. He knew it was an angel and that he would be all right.

I wonder if and how it changed his life? Or did he like so many others put the experience into a corner of his mind and shut the door?

Before we come into incarnation, we discuss our life purpose with the Lords of Karma, those in the angel hierarchy who oversee our balance sheets of accountability. We choose our time of birth according to the availability of appropriate parents for the experience we need. We decide on the planetary aspects that will affect us. More evolved souls are more careful about the conditions for their incarnation and therefore fewer choices are available to them.

We predetermine the length of our life and the time of our departure. The latter decision can be varied by certain choices during our lifetime. If, for instance, we allow our physical body to fall into disrepair by bad diet, it may no longer be able comfortably to house our spirit. If we lose the will to live, we may leave before our time. Of course, suicide is often a premature way of opting out of our mission on Earth but there are many forms of suicide. People drink themselves to death. They take ridiculous risks against their intuition. They die of a broken heart. They send out such powerfully negative thoughts that they become ill. We can only die before our chosen span if we are wilful enough. Angels can only help us within the framework of free will.

If we abort our mission on Earth, we have to re-do it with similar circumstances and challenges. If we leave ten years early for instance before we complete one last karmic repayment, we may only need to come back to this planet for ten years to repay the debt. In that case we will die in our next life as a child. The angels will support us whatever we choose.

However, if it is definitely not our time to die, then our angel will save us. They may even do this in a physical way. There are many reports of people feeling a rush of warm air and finding themselves being pushed by an unseen force out of danger.

There was a wartime expression that if a bullet had your number on it your time was up. If it was not your time you were safe. The angels were protecting you.

More and more people are reporting near-death experiences. Throughout cultures and religions these stories are remarkably consistent. The most commonly reported is that in which someone is moving along a tunnel of light with a wonderful sense of peace and love but an angel, a being of light or a voice tells them their task is not finished and they must return to complete it.

In other cases an angel or shining wise person, who is presumably a representative of the Lords of Karma, takes them to review their situation and offers them a choice to return and change their lives.

There are no accidental deaths
for our angels will rescue us
if it is not our time to leave the planet.

CHAPTER 30

Angel Wisdom

Angels serve spirit. True spirituality is beyond religion, though it accepts and honours all despite the fact that most religions have moved far from the pure message of spirit.

True spirituality looks at a mountain and sees that every path up to Source is right for the person climbing it — even pain and disease, even hurt and disaster are pathways. The pain, the disease, the hurt, the disaster are often the challenges which turn people to spirit. The deepest despair is often the pit from which people call out to spirit for help.

Those who unconsciously work for the darkness, sadly often in the name of God and religion, seek to control, constrict or disempower others. They may say, "You will only reach the mountain top if you do it this way". They may even refuse to help someone out of a situation unless the person follows their path. This is control and manipulation, narrowmindedness and lack of compassion. If anyone tries to restrict or imprison another in the name of the light, they do a terrible disservice to the planet and, of course, bear awful karma for it.

God-fearing people walk in the dark. God-loving people grow towards the light.

Angel-fearing people live in the shadow. Angel-loving people dance with joy.

To promote ignorance keeps the light from people. Those who knowingly conceal the truth or distort it on the pretext that the masses are not ready to hear it, serve the darkness. Throughout history, sacred and esoteric texts have been hidden away or destroyed.

In AD 553 at the Second Council of Constantinople, the Emperor Justinian had reincarnation written out of the Bible. He and the church wanted to claim power over people's souls. When this information is brought to light, and the sacred Laws of Reincarnation are recognised, people will at last be in charge of their own destinies. They will no longer give authority to intermediaries in the religious hierarchies to tell them what they may or may not do on their path to the light.

When this truth is revealed each one of us will know that our every action is recorded by our guardian angel in the akashic records and that we ourselves can take charge of our destiny.

Do not feel angry and frustrated as you read this. Rather calmly ask the angels to help bring the truth to light. Ask them to open the minds of those in charge of controlling the masses on the planet. Ask them to light up the religious and world leaders.

Religions tell people what to do and what to believe. Spirituality tells people to listen for their own guidance and follow their hearts. It leaves people free, reminding us only of the highest qualities like harmlessness, love, joy, compassion, integrity, brotherhood, sisterhood, peace and oneness. Even saying these words ignites a light within us.

Anyone who preaches hellfire and damnation is energising the darkness and therefore working for it. These preachers add to the fear in our Universe. Every single time we say the names which personalise the devil, the vibration of the name increases his power. Even swearing has a vibration which lowers our potential.

At the beginning of the fifteenth century, the priesthood was tainted with corruption. When this happened the priests stopped defending the angels, the light. Instead they attacked the devil and energized it, allowing the horrors of the Inquisition to take place. However when they killed the witches, they were in reality killing the healers, the seers and prophets and those of the truth. Many of these souls are now reincarnating to bring the light back to Earth.

A truly spiritual person will trust others to find their own way to the top of the mountain and will assist impartially. If someone wants to move to a different path, an enlightened being will wish them well. A spiritual being will not judge someone who takes a wrong turn. He or she will encourage others to think for themselves, to listen to their inner guidance and be independent. They will empower everyone to speak directly to Source or angels or Beings of Higher Wisdom.

Angels of light will help anyone climbing any path up that mountain. All are equal. And even if some are slithering downwards, angels will still patiently stand by without judgement to help when they are asked.

People sometimes ask how it is that angels speak so many different languages. Most of us are telepathic. We often pick up what other people are thinking and usually we say in surprise, "Oh, I was just thinking that!" Beyond the limitations of the body, in the higher realms, all communication is telepathic. Words are not needed because the energy of what is being communicated is transferred to the other person. This is not done haphazardly and unconsciously in the way we tend to do it. Rather as a message is formed by the sender, it is directed in a stream of consciousness to the recipient.

When angels and higher beings communicate with us they direct a stream of consciousness to us which reaches us as a powerful thought or voice in our head. Sound may be added to create a voice. However, it is the energy which is transferred and then filtered through our consciousness in our language. So angels do not need to be linguists. They communicate in the language of the Creator, the vibration of love.

At the first angel workshop I ran, I was guiding a meditation. I was clearly told that we were all being too analytical and must stop thinking Instead we must fill our minds with the colour white-violet. Immediately I felt an immense white-violet light flame in my third eye. I had the most incredible sensation of peace and oneness. Afterwards I discovered that many had felt this same powerful feeling as the angels came closer. To immerse ourselves in the colour white-violet or violet will increase our vibratory rate.

So there are five ways to connect more closely with angels of light.

1. Think about them frequently. Ask them to come closer and help.

2. Cleanse and purify your thoughts so that your auric field is more penetrable to their fine vibration.

3. Stop analysing and overthinking everything. This puts you in your left brain and prevents the connection. Whenever you find yourself in your heads, place a white-violet light in your minds.

4. Be receptive to their presence and their messages.

5. Listen to angel music. This is now being channelled by a number of sources. It refines your vibrations allowing angels to penetrate your aura. It is truly beautiful. How do you know if it is genuine? How do you know if it is right for you? Use your intuition.

Angels help you claim authority over your own soul.

CHAPTER 31

Inspiration

One day I was sitting quietly thinking about the many problems that people I knew were facing. Suddenly an angelic voice impressed itself. It said, "The reason so many of you are going through challenges is because karma is speeding up. You must face your demons, learn your lessons and move on. There is no time for rests now."

Karma is the inevitable repayment of our debts. If we have ever thought or done something to hurt or harm another, we have to repay. There is no escaping the consequence of our actions for the balance sheet of karma runs throughout our soul's experience, often over many lifetimes.

I had been going through a period of difficulty myself. Even though I was trying to keep centred and steady through this challenge, I knew that my emotions were fluctuating.

"How can we help and heal others when we feel like this?" I questioned.

The angelic voice replied, "Get out of your personality into your golden body. It is your angelic body."

I smiled when it said that. The golden body is an expression I use to mean a state of centred detachment. The expression originated some years ago when I was working with a clairvoyant client who looked at me and said with a gasp, "Oh, you are completely golden. You're in your golden body."

When we shift gear into our golden body we are in a space in which nothing and no one outside us can affect us. We leave our personality behind so we are listening to higher guidance and are totally focused on what we are doing.

The voice continued with what was totally astonishing information to me, "Because this is an especially difficult time now, angels are moving close to planet Earth to help. Your atoms, cells and DNA are being changed, so that you can enter the fifth dimension. You may feel the sensations in your body — in your heart, shoulders, solar plexus and new budding chakras. You humans are multidimensional. Angels are fifth-dimensional and above."

Most human beings have been living in a physical world where we believe in the existence of only that which we can see, feel and touch. We have been living in a material world, limited by our beliefs.

We constantly need love and approval from others. We fear rejection, abandonment and aloneness. This means that we humans try to control and manipulate others to get these needs met. Needing physical, mental and emotional support leads to co-dependent relationships. Such relationships stunt our spiritual growth.

When we do turn to spirit, most of us ask for things we want or for our needs to be met.

Planet Earth is to become a fifth-dimensional planet, which is a planet of higher consciousness. In this state of consciousness we do not need support or approval from other humans, so we no longer seek co-dependent relationships. Our sole aim is to follow our highest spiritual purpose.

At the higher dimension we are living at a greater level of trust, so when we ask for something from God or Source we expect to receive. In any case we are focused on asking for the development of qualities rather than things.

In the fifth dimension we will live in a state of harmony,

peace and detachment, working for the highest good of ourselves and all others.

No wonder angels with all their love and wisdom are flocking near to planet Earth to help in this massive shift in consciousness!

The voice continued, "You can connect with angels more easily when you are in a fifth-dimensional body, which is your golden body. Moving into this higher state of consciousness is like shifting gear. Most of you do it automatically but there are things that help.

* *Read inspirational books. This will keep you open to spirit.*
* *Focus on beauty, joy and higher qualities.*
* *Walk in and enjoy nature as often as you can.*
* *Listen to inspirational music. Music enters your cells and lifts your vibratory levels.*
* *Constantly say thank you for the things that you do have. When you say thank you, you send out an energy of appreciation which attracts more good things into your life.*
* *Relax. We know this is difficult when you feel you are hurtling along in the river of life but we ask you to trust and let the flow take you.*

I asked how to connect with angels. The voice replied, "Simply focus on angels!"

To bring angels into your life,
focus on angels.

CHAPTER 32

Angel Exercises

I end this book with some guided journeys to help you to become closer to your angels and allow them to help you in ways which you may never have thought possible.

Make sure that you are wearing comfortable clothing and will not be disturbed for half an hour.

To raise the energy in the room you may care to light a candle and have crystals, plants or flowers around you. Spiritual books in the room also help to lift the vibrations in order to connect with angels, as does beautiful music.

Before you start your meditation, put out the intention that whatever happens is for your highest good. Ask for the angels of light to come to you to protect and heal you.

To meet your angel

1. Sit or lie comfortably.

2. Breathe slightly more deeply than usual, relaxing on the outbreath until your whole body feels calm.

3. Invite your guardian angel to come close. Feel its gentle wings enfold you and relax into the safety.

4. Ask your guardian angel its name. Rejoice if its name comes into your mind but don't worry if it doesn't.

5. Enfolded in the love and security of your guardian angel, become aware of other angels around you and how much love each has for you.

6. Breathe in all the love available to you. Remind yourself you deserve to be loved.

7. When you are ready open your eyes gently.

To cleanse and heal your heart

1. Sit or lie comfortably.

2. Take a deep breath and, as you let it out, centre yourself. Then on each outbreath, say 'calm' to yourself, until you feel really relaxed.

3. Sense the outside of your heart. Is it smooth and healthy or is it rough, bruised, cracked, broken or hurt in any way?

4. Sense inside your heart. Is it full of love or is it full of hurt, anger or jealousy? Are there old unresolved incidents stuck in there waiting to be healed?

5. Invite healing angels to come to heal your heart and sense how many come to help you.

6. Allow them to soothe, mend or heal your heart in whatever way they wish to.

7. Let them take out your heart and carry it up to a beautiful cascade. As they hold your heart in the water, sense and watch the old hurts wash away.

8. The angels are carrying your heart up to Source now for a blessing. Relax and be receptive and open to anything that may happen.

9. Send thanks for anything you have received.

10. Open up to allow your purified and blessed heart to be re- turned into your body.

11. Sense the angels stroking your aura, so that you are closed down and safe.

12. When you are ready, open your eyes and focus on loving thoughts.

To meet the Lords of Karma

The Lords of Karma help us to make our life choices. They keep the akashic records, which are our balance sheets of good and bad. They will give us help and guidance if we ask for it. If you have a challenge in your life about which you wish to ask for guidance, you may like to decide on a question before you start your journey.

1. Take several deep breaths and as you release them, say 'peace' to yourself.

2. Starting with your toes, relax your body all the way to your crown.

3. Invite your angel to come close and sense or watch it coming to you. Take a moment to greet it lovingly.

4. Ask it to conduct you up to the Lords of Karma for help and guidance.

5. Let it take you by the hand and draw you up through the clouds, the stars and through the Universe.

6. Breathe in light and breathe out jealousy, anger, guilt, hurt or fear. Take your time doing this.

7. Ahead of you is a beautiful white temple. Let your angel take you up the white steps and across the courtyard to the door of the room where the Lords of Karma are seated.

8. Knock and ask permission to enter. Then approach the Lords of Karma humbly and calmly.

9. Ask your question or ask for guidance to help you release karma.

10. Await a response. Even if nothing appears to happen, your request will have been noted and guidance will come as soon as you are ready to receive it.

11. Thank the Lords of Karma for admitting you and allow your angel to bring you back down to Earth.

12. Thank your angel and rest quietly before opening your eyes.

To bring higher qualities into your life

In the Age of Aquarius, the new golden age, which we have just entered, we will live at a higher level of consciousness. Instead of focusing on the material world, it will be our joy and delight to increase higher qualities in our lives. These may be freedom, peace, love, enthusiasm, gratitude, balance, beauty or any number of wonderful qualities which make us feel good.

One way to start this process is to invite the angels to increase in our lives the qualities we wish to focus on. This exercise will draw the angels close to you to help you do this.

1. Sit quietly and calmly. Breathe in light and breathe out love until you feel relaxed and still.

2. Decide on one or two higher qualities you would like to increase in your life.

3. Invite in your guardian angel and feel it enfold and support you.

4. For a few moments think of one of the qualities you wish to have more of.

5. Invite in the angel of that quality. You may see or have an impression of this angel, its colour, its size, the way it is dressed.

6. Ask the angel to bring more of this quality into your life.

7. See, sense, feel your life filled with this higher quality.

8. Expect more of this quality to come to you.

9. Open your eyes.

To release fears

Angels are willing and ready to help us to let go of old fears if we will only relax and trust them to do so.

1. Relax and breathe calmly and evenly.

2. Invite an angel in to help you release your fear and the tension it causes in your body.

3. You may like to think about your fear or simply breathe into the tense part of your body where you hold the fear.

4. Allow a picture, memory or symbol to float into your mind.

5. Relax while the angel or angels pull the picture, memory or symbol from you. Allow them to dissolve the fear in light.

6. They will now show you a positive picture or symbol which will help you to feel strong.

7. They are placing this symbol either into your third eye or into the part of your body which was tense.

8. Thank your angels and open your eyes.

To increase self-worth and confidence

Our solar plexus is the seat of our lower will. It is here that we hold our sense of self-worth and confidence. Many people hold fear here. The angels are willing to help you release this now to enhance your confidence and sense of value.

1. Relax and be still.

2. Breathe into your solar plexus with long, slow, deep, even breaths.

3. Imagine you are going into your solar plexus and finding a cellar or a room. What is it like?

4. Invite your angel to take out any old memories, fears or negativities.

5. Allow your angel to pull out any darkness or dirt or dust.

6. Be aware of your angel making you a golden ball of light and filling it with confidence, worth and power.

7. Be receptive as it places this golden ball of energy into your solar plexus.

8. Breathe into it and feel your value and worth increasing.

9. Thank your angel and open your eyes.

Freedom from attachment

We cannot enjoy anything if we are attached to it because we fear we will be unhappy if we lose it. This applies to material possessions, hobbies, jobs and sometimes even qualities such as anger. So in the new consciousness it is fine to have things as long as we are clear our ego does not need them.

It is the same with people. Need of any description forms cords which attach us to people and cause us to manipulate them emotionally. Unconditional love forms no cords and leaves others totally free to be themselves.

The angels are willing to help us release, uncord and set ourselves and others free.

1. Let your whole body relax and become comfortable and at ease.

2. Decide what or who you are now ready to release.

3. See or sense it or them in front of you.

4. Be aware of whatever links you to it.

5. Invite an angel in to sever the link and dissolve the cords right to the roots. Be aware you may feel this in your physical body.

6. Ask the angel to fill you with a higher quality to help you let this go from your life.

7. Breathe in the higher quality.

8. Thank the angel and open your eyes.

To heal your inner child

Most of us have an inner child who is stuck or lost and hurting. Whenever we have pain in our body we can be sure that our inner child is telling us that it is in pain and causing disruption in our energy flow.

When we feel hurt, frightened, angry, jealous, envious, obstinate or not good enough, there is a part of us still stuck in childhood, creating problems in our life.

The angels are very happy to help us heal these stuck parts of ourselves if we ask them to.

1. Take a few moments to loosen the joints of your body and relax.

2. Breathe comfortably into your tummy, expanding it, and then slowly release the breath. Repeat this several times until you begin to feel very comfortable.

3. Remember the last time you felt angry, hurt or negative in any way. Be aware that the balanced wise adult is not feeling these emotions. The emotions are those of your stuck child. Sense how old is this child within you.

4. When you find the child, comfort it and invite in the healing angels to heal it.

5. Relax and be open to whatever the angels do to heal the child.

6. When they return your child to you notice how different it looks and feels.

7. Thank the angels.

8. Hold and love your inner child.

To heal your ancestors

So much pain and hurt is passed down through generations. So many unresolved family patterns continue down the line. These are the issues which keep too many souls stuck in the heavy energy field around planet Earth causing them to reincarnate again and again.

Angels are ready and willing to help us release ourselves and our ancestors.

1. Breathe down into your feet until they feel heavy and comfortable. Then breathe down into your legs until they too feel very relaxed. Do the same with your hands, your arms, your back and your trunk.

2. Invite the appropriate angels to come to you and relax in their wonderful energy.

3. Explain to the angels what the pattern is you need help with.

4. Have a sense of the line of ancestors all carrying the burden of this pattern.

5. Allow the angels to lift you up through the Universe, higher and higher until you can see a radiant white light. Within this light is Source.

6. With the angels, kneel and ask for grace for yourself and your ancestors.

7. A symbol will be given to you if grace is granted.

8. Return down to Earth with the symbol and pass it back along the line of ancestors.

9. Thank the angels and open your eyes.

FEB 0 . 2009